ZION
THE GROWING SYMBOL

A Case Study Approach On Images of Zion

Edited by David Premoe

Pastoral Services Commission
The Auditorium, P.O. Box 1059
Independence, Missouri 64051

Reorganized CHURCH OF JESUS CHRIST of Latter Day Saints

Copyright © 1980
HERALD PUBLISHING HOUSE
Independence, Missouri
Printed in the United States of America

10 9 8 7 6 5 4 3 2

TABLE OF CONTENTS

Case Study One: The White Oak Street Church   8
Chapter One: The Gospel and the Human Condition 12
       by Geoffrey F. Spencer
Case Study Two: The Campaign of Howard Wilson 20
Chapter Two: Zion in Scripture and History 22
       by Geoffrey F. Spencer
Case Study Three: The Jackson and Cooper Families . . . 30
Chapter Three: Historical Images of Zion 33
       by Richard P. Howard
Case Study Four: The Shepherd Congregation 42
Chapter Four: Images of Zion in the Reorganization . . . 45
       by Richard P. Howard
Case Study Five: The Wimbleton Congregation
                  and the Reentry Project 52
Chapter Five: Zion, the Kingdom of God, and the World 56
       by Geoffrey F. Spencer
Case Study Six: The Marion County Bond Issue 65
Chapter Six: Zion as Response, Incarnation, and Power . 68
       by Joe A. Serig
Case Study Seven: Sister Jones 76
Chapter Seven: Zion as Symbol 79
       by Geoffrey F. Spencer
Case Study Eight: Mary Davidson 88
Chapter Eight: Zion as Process 92
       by Geoffrey F. Spencer

Case Study Nine: Sam Jones.....................100
Chapter Nine: Zion as a Stewardship Response........103
    by Geoffrey F. Spencer
Case Study Ten: Jan and Jim Burns.................111
Chapter Ten: Zion as Anticipating the Future........115
    by Geoffrey F. Spencer

EDITOR'S NOTE

The belief in Zion as the call to become the corporate expression of God's redeeming love has been historically a central focus for the Restoration movement. From its earliest beginnings, the Latter Day Saint Church has been seeking ways to give concrete expression to this belief. Over the years the image of Zion has grown as each generation adds its own understandings. Each new understanding has been a reflection of the period out of which it has come. Consequently, Zion has acquired a variety of meanings that in some cases seem to be in conflict. With this in mind, *Zion: The Growing Symbol* has been produced to help the reader review and better understand images of Zion from the past and to become aware of images that are growing in the soils of current history.

Each of the ten chapters of this booklet is divided into two parts. The first part is a case study. The case studies, written by David Premoe, are designed to raise some of the primary issues the chapters will be discussing. The second part of each chapter is an article that focuses on a particular image related to an understanding of Zion. The articles have been written by three authors. Seven were written by Geoffrey Spencer and were initially presented at the Asia-Pacific Conference of 1978. Two were written by Richard Howard for the January 1976 edition of *Commission* magazine. The remaining article was written by Joe Serig and first appeared in the 1978 reunion resource. The booklet has been designed as a twenty-lesson adult study text. Each case study and each article has study questions for promoting discussion. It is recommended that one lesson concentrate on a case and the next on the corresponding article.

As the Reorganized Church of Jesus Christ of Latter Day Saints moves through the decade of the eighties with the "Faith to Grow" it will be important to understand the growth in vision that the church has experienced regarding Zion. Such understanding can better equip the Saints to be involved in the further growth and expansion of the cause of Zion in the world. For this reason *Zion: The Growing Symbol* has been produced.

David Premoe

CASE STUDY ONE

THE WHITE OAK STREET CONGREGATION

The White Oak Street congregation of the Saints Church is facing a critical decision. Twenty-five years ago members of the original congregation built a church building on White Oak Street on the growing edge of a large city. At that time it was felt that the surrounding neighborhood would provide an excellent setting for a church. Many church members lived in the surrounding neighborhood and the area was considered an ideal place for witnessing. In the early years of the congregation's life the church became a fairly significant part of the neighborhood. Some of the neighbors began to attend church at White Oak Street and some were eventually baptized.

But as the years passed and the city expanded, the neighborhood surrounding the White Oak Street Church began to change. Many of the people who had lived there when the church was built began moving farther out to newer suburbs. They were replaced by lower income families who were moving out from the inner city. Gradually the neighborhood was transformed from a middle income suburb to a low income section of the inner city.

Now, twenty-five years later, the members of the White Oak Street congregation find themselves going to church in a neighborhood occupied by people with whom they have little in common. Consequently, the church presently has little or no significance for the people who live around it or the people who attend it. The building has been vandalized more than once in the past year. On Sunday morning the neighborhood children who play ball in the church parking lot have to be sent away so that people can park. Generally, there is a great deal of outside noise that intrudes on the spirit of worship within.

Recently, the congregation has been approached by another religious group with an offer to purchase the White Oak Street Church building. About half of the members of the congregation favor accepting the offer and relocating in a different area. The other half would rather investigate the possibility of staying on White Oak Street and finding appropriate ways to bring ministry to the surrounding neighborhood. Thus the White Oak Street congregation is trying to decide whether to stay in a neighborhood where they have little in common or move to another area.

Additional Facts About the Congregation

1. None of the members of the congregation presently attending the White Oak Street Church live in the neighborhood where the church is located. Many drive a considerable distance to attend.

2. Most of the members of the congregation are middle-income suburban dwellers with very little experience in relating to low-income urban dwellers.

3. The church building as a facility is in good condition and adequately equipped to meet the needs of the current membership. The church also owns the lot adjacent to it, providing space for future expansion.

4. The church building is completely paid for and the congregation has a small accumulation of savings in its building fund.

Additional Facts About the Neighborhood

1. The neighborhood does not have any form of neighborhood association.

2. The neighborhood does not have any organized programs for children.

3. The neighborhood has one or two outspoken people who are pushing for improvements within the neighborhood.

4. The people living in the neighborhood know very little about the White Oak Street Church and generally ignore it.

Based on the information given in the case study of the White Oak Street Church consider the following questions.
1. What are the primary issues involved in making the decision to stay or move? List the factors that make moving seem like a good choice. List the factors that make staying seem like a good choice.

2. There are times when people feel less free to function because of uncertainties, fears, or alienations. What are some of the possible uncertainties, fears, or alienations that members of the White Oak Street congregation are facing as they struggle to make their decision? What are some of the possible uncertainties, fears, or alienations that the people in the

neighborhood are experiencing in relationship to the White Oak Street Church?

3. If you were a member of the White Oak Street congregation, what would you choose to do? Explain your choice.

4. How well do you know the neighborhood where your church is located? List all of the characteristics you can think of about this neighborhood. How many members of the congregation reside in the neighborhood where the church is located? List those characteristics that you feel the congregation and the neighborhood have in common.

5. Make a list of services that you feel your congregation has to offer the neighborhood where the church is located.

CHAPTER ONE

THE GOSPEL AND THE HUMAN CONDITION

by Geoffrey F. Spencer

And this is the gospel, the glad tidings which the voice out of the heavens bore record unto us, that he came into the world, even Jesus to be crucified for the world, and to bear the sins of the world, and to sanctify the world.—Doctrine and Covenants 76:4g.

In the New Testament the gospel is the good news that God has entered into the world in the person of his Son for its redemption. The gospel is the good news that God, who is the creator of all, loves his creation. The gospel is good news because it speaks to our human condition with the assurance that there is a truth about God, about ourselves, about the nature of the universe, and about the purpose of life which is cause for hope rather than despair, for joy rather than sorrow.

Jesus Christ is the revelation of God's action in the world and the means by which we know of the depth of God's love for persons. John's gospel states the message quite clearly: "For God so loved the world, that he gave his Only Begotten Son, that whosoever believeth on him should not perish; but have everlasting life. For God sent not his Son into the world to condemn the world; but that the world through him might be saved" (John 3:16-17). Repeatedly, the scriptures bear witness that the love of God is revealed in the life of the man, Jesus of

Nazareth. Thus the Christian can speak with assurance of the love of God because the scriptures and the presence of the Holy Spirit bear witness that the love of God and the love of Christ are one and the same: "God [was] in Christ, reconciling the world unto himself" (II Corinthians 5:19).

Thus the good news is not, in the first place, in the form of a message in words or a series of doctrines. Essentially the good news is in the event of Jesus, who by his birth, life, death, and resurrection is known to us as Lord. The gospel is the good news that "Jesus is the Christ." Jesus is more than the bearer of good news; he is himself the good announced. This is the meaning of the announcement by John that "the Word was made flesh."

Again, the gospel is not primarily a commandment that we be good or that we obey a certain number of commandments. Rather, it is the revelation that God's goodness reaches out to establish a new relationship with us by which we can safely commit ourselves to him. Faith is the gift of God within us which enables us to commit ourselves without fear or reservation.

It appears to be part of our situation that we try to find freedom by our own means or by "justifying" ourselves. Human beings will attempt to establish their own merit by priding themselves on their achievements, their virtue, or some other characteristic. At times groups of persons have claimed worth because of their race, national identity, or color, or because of some superior endowment of intelligence or skill. Judaism in the time of Jesus claimed merit on the grounds of obedience to the Law. The witness of the apostle Paul is that all such attempts to justify ourselves are vain and ultimately unsatisfying.

As humankind lives in this condition, we experience *bondage*. The reality of that bondage is experienced by every person. It may help us to think of this condition being faced in the six concrete relationships of life. Three of these relationships are temporal: the imagined *future*, the remembered *past*, and the experienced *now*. The other three are personal relationships: to *God*, to *self*, and to *neighbor*.

In each of these relationships we experience our bondage. In reference to the future, we experience the bondage which is *anxiety*. In remembering the past we experience the bondage of *guilt*. In relation to the present we find it difficult to discover a meaning to life and experience the bondage of *meaninglessness*. In some societies this may be experienced as *boredom*. In each of our personal relationships we experience the bondage of *alienation:* with reference to our neighbors we are *lonely* or *separated*; our relation with self is often *despairing*, and our relation to God is fraught with *idolatry*.

The effect of these distorted relationships is enslavement. We experience a bondage from which it is impossible to free ourselves. Whatever way we believe we can free ourselves turns out to be the source of despair, frustration, and defeat. It must be, according to the scriptures, God who justifies us.

The biblical image of God is that of Deliverer. The "good news" of the gospel is that God in Jesus Christ has acted for our deliverance, and it is his intention that we shall know this truth and be set free (John 8:32). In each relationship where we have suffered bondage, the gospel creates the experience of freedom. Instead of experiencing the future as dread or anxiety, we anticipate it in hope. By the good news of *forgiveness*, the disabling power of guilt is lifted and we can receive our past without feeling condemned by it. Our relationship to the present is also redeemed in Christ. The world's present existence is affirmed as *meaningful* because God himself has participated in it.

The gospel is also good news in terms of our experience of ourselves. We are delivered from the "old man" to become "new creatures" in Christ. In relation to others, we find ourselves *reconciled*, so that barriers and suspicions are broken down. In relation to God, we are saved from the idolatry which worships things and causes of secondary importance, and related to God in *faith*.

Put in the form of a diagram, this is how we may think of the gospel redeeming our condition of bondage:

LIFE'S RELATIONSHIPS	PREDICAMENT (Bondage)	NEW POSSIBILITY IN THE GOSPEL (Freedom)
TEMPORAL		
Future	Dread, Anxiety	Hope
Past	Guilt	Forgiveness
Present	Meaninglessness, Boredom	Meaningfulness
PERSONAL		
God	Idolatry	Faith
Others	Separation, Loneliness	Reconciliation
Self	Despair	Newness, Hope

What is the outcome of such freedom as we experience in the gospel? In the assurance that God loves us, that we can love ourselves, and that we can risk loving others, we find *joy*. We discover that we can experience our lives as a gift rather than a burden and are moved to *gratitude*. We find a new sense of *community* with others, not because we are better than, or more clever than, or achieve more than others but because we have all shared the experience of being forgiven and accepted by the love of God.

Finally, we are moved to make an appropriate *response*, not out of fear or out of the desire to earn our way but because the love of God has demanded a commitment. One way in which we may think about *Zion* has to do with the nature of our response to the grace of God as a community of persons who are finding freedom through the good news of the gospel. Joe Serig describes the idea of Zion in this way:

> **One key idea about Zion... is that Zion is essentially a collective response to God's love. Zion, then, becomes a type of corporate repentance whereby persons who have individually committed their lives to God through his Son Jesus Christ join in trying to shape and change the value systems of communities. Thus those communities can more nearly reflect the basic ethic of love of God and love of fellow beings in all relationships. Just as the concept of stewardship is a recognition that we return to God a portion of the gift that has been bestowed upon us for the welfare of others, so Zion is a collective response to the awareness that all of life is a gift from God. When Zion is seen as a response to divine grace, opportunities for repentance, reconciliation, and expressions of universal**

brotherhood and sisterhood become tangible evidences of our commitment to God.*

CHAPTER ONE STUDY QUESTIONS

1. How does the chapter define the term "gospel"? If the members of the White Oak Street Church decide to remain there what are some ways that they can make the gospel relevant to the surrounding neighborhood?

2. The chapter describes several ways in which people experience bondage—anxiety, guilt, meaninglessness, idolatry, separation, despair. If they elect to stay, what kinds of anxiety might the members of the White Oak Street Church experience as they anticipate the future? What are the possible elements of hope that could help relieve the anxiety?

3. What kind of anxieties do you experience as you anticipate the future of your own congregation? What are your hopes for the future that help relieve the anxieties?

4. One definition of Zion in the chapter describes Zion as "People together with a common conviction responding to the assurance that *all* life is a gift of God." What does this definition mean to you? How

---

*Richard D. Hughes, "Zion Building: Seek Ye First to Build Up the Kingdom," *Zion as Response, Incarnation, and Power*, Joe A. Serig, Independence, Mo., Herald House, 1978, pp. 16-17.

might this definition be applied to the situation of the White Oak Street congregation? How might this definition be interpreted in terms of your own congregation?

5. Make a list of ways that your congregation can make the gospel relevant to the surrounding neighborhood.

6. What primary learnings have you experienced from reading the chapter?

CASE STUDY TWO

THE CAMPAIGN OF HOWARD WILSON

In the election year of 1992, Howard Wilson, a member of the RLDS Church, is running for the office of mayor of the city of Independence, Missouri. Howard has been a city council member for the past four years and has served the city well. As the main part of his campaign, Howard is visiting RLDS churches in Independence to solicit the support of the Saints. Whenever he is invited to speak in one of the churches his remarks are always the same. His speech goes something like this:

Friends, I am here this evening as a member with you in God's church, to ask for your help. I believe that the time is not far off when our Lord Jesus Christ will return to earth to claim his kingdom. As you all know, the scriptures tell us that the kingdom will begin here in Zion among God's chosen people. We have been admonished to prepare ourselves for that great time. As the Church of Jesus Christ in these latter days, we have also been called to be in the forefront. The time has come to prepare the city of Independence for the day when the cause of Zion will be established. Our people are called to be in the forefront of this preparation. This means that the Saints must begin moving into the authority roles in our community to place the church in a better position to bring God's influence to bear. For these reasons I have decided to run for the office of mayor of the city of Independence. As one of God's children who has been chosen to take part in the building of his kingdom, I am here to ask for your vote. Thank you and may God bless our efforts.

Based on the information given in this case study consider the following questions:

1. What are the verbal images used by Howard Wilson to talk about the church, Independence, and Zion?

What image of Zion is Howard Wilson projecting? How does this image fit with your view of Zion?

2. Do you agree with Howard Wilson that the Saints are called to be in the forefront? How do you respond to the way he is pursuing this call? How do you interpret the idea of "being in the forefront"? In what ways can your congregation be in the forefront of your community?

3. How does Howard Wilson use the term *chosen* in terms of the church? Do you agree with his view of the church and its members being chosen? Explain.

4. In your opinion, is it legitimate for Howard Wilson, as a concerned member of the church, to run for political office? If you were advising Wilson on his campaign strategy, what would you recommend?

5. What effect does Howard Wilson's campaign speech have on you? What effect do you think his campaign speech has on the non-RLDS members of the community?

CHAPTER TWO

ZION IN SCRIPTURE AND HISTORY

by Geoffrey F. Spencer

In Christian history, as well as in some other religious traditions, the hope of realizing the fulfillment of human hopes on earth has been a very powerful idea. This has been especially true of those religious faiths which teach that human history is the place where our destiny is worked out and that what happens in history is an expression of the divine will for humankind. For Christians this hope has been expressed in the belief in the kingdom of God.

In the Old Testament, the hope in God's perfect kingdom coming to rule over humankind was expressed in very specific ways. Israel saw itself as the Lord's chosen people, responsible by a covenant to God for being the means by which the kingdom would be established and "Zion" raised as an example to the world. The Israelites were inspired by the vision of paradise coming down from heaven to be achieved on earth. God was exclusively the God of the nation of Israel, and Jerusalem would be a place both of protection and of great blessings. Thus the kingdom of the Old Testament was an exclusive kingdom, involving the chosen nation and centering in the city of Jerusalem.

As this dream began to fade, the Old Testament prophets looked to the future as the time when God would institute his kingdom on earth. The golden age of King David would be restored in even greater splendor by the expected Messiah (Isaiah 9:6-7) and God would put a new law in the hearts of the people (Jeremiah 31:33). Moreover, when God's kingdom, the new Zion or the New Jerusalem, was established it would be an example to all the world.

And it shall come to pass in the last days, when the mountain of the Lord's house shall be established in the top of the mountains, and shall be exalted above the hills, and all nations shall flow unto it; and many people shall go and say, Come ye, and let us go up to the mountain of the Lord... and he will teach us of his ways... for out of Zion shall go forth the law, and the word of the Lord from Jerusalem.—Isaiah 2:2-3.

It is out of this long tradition and hope for God's reign on Mount Zion that we understand why many people in the time of Jesus, including his closest disciples, expected that he, as the Messiah, would overthrow the existing government and set up a new political kingdom. Certainly the coming kingdom was central to the message of Jesus:

...Jesus came into Galilee, preaching the gospel of the kingdom of God; and saying, The time is fulfilled, and the kingdom of God is at hand; repent ye, and believe the gospel.—Mark 1:12-13.

Even after the resurrection, the disciples asked Jesus, "Lord, wilt thou at this time restore again the kingdom to Israel?" This suggests that the disciples had not fully understood the nature of the kingdom which Jesus preached and which he said was "at hand" or "among you." In fact, it was the refusal of Jesus to accept this cultural expectation of establishing a literal kingdom with political power which eventually resulted in his crucifixion. People who wanted a concrete earthly kingdom supported by military strength could not understand the meaning and the power of the new covenant of love, sacrificial service, and suffering. But this was the nature of the kingdom which Jesus said was "not of this world."

It is important to recognize that the early settlements in the land of America, and the establishment of the United States of America, were very much influenced by the idea of the promised land. The terms "Zion," "New Jerusalem," and the "city set on a hill" were widely used among early Americans, and they tended to see their nation as called to fulfill God's divine purpose to establish a new Zion, far away from Europe which they considered to be fallen and beyond redemption. The early Puritan settlers believed that the kingdom of God would soon be reestablished and that the Lord would return to reign over his American Israel. There was in America a combination of the hope of the early Christian church that the resurrected Lord would return to reign over his kingdom and the Old Testament idea that the kingdom would be a specific place with a divine political rule. In fact, in some of the colonies only those who were baptized members of the church were permitted to vote in elections.

The early Latter Day Saint movement was very deeply influenced by these ideas of God's coming kingdom on earth, and by the conviction of the special destiny for America. While Independence was generally referred to as the "Center Place" there was a strong tendency, especially toward the latter part of Joseph Smith's life, for the prophet to think of the whole of America as the land of Zion. Zion was thought of not only as the gathering place for the righteous Saints who would "come out of Babylon" but also as a place of refuge and safety, and as a place for the Saints to greet the returning Lord.

Much of the persecution experienced by the early Latter Day Saints grew out of the suspicions of their neighbors that the Saints were trying to create a government of their own. In fact, Zion was seen by many members, especially as the main body of Saints moved to Nauvoo, as an independent "chosen people" or "latter-day Israel" with their own political system and power. We would say today that not only was such a hope unacceptable within a sovereign state such as the United States of America but that it was not in harmony with the way in which Christ had called disciples to share his mission in the world. Christ had rejected the idea of an exclusive community which would be separated from the rest of the world or that would be a sign to the world. He reminded members of the early church that they were to be the light, the salt, and the leaven at work within the nations of the world. Their mission was to go into all the world, teaching people to observe all things and baptizing in his name.

Alan Tyree has written some comments about the way in which we might think about Zion today, and how we might see all cultures sharing in the challenge of working with God and with each other to establish the cause of Zion. His words help us to see how the cause of Zion can be a great endeavor and source of blessing for all nations, rather than for just one favored nation.

Probably for most of our members, Zion is thought of as a community on a sacred piece of geography, dominated by Lat-

ter Day Saint influence, and characterized by a perfection of social, governmental, and economic relationships. It is seen as an end or a goal, rather than as a means or a process.

There are two different scriptural images of Zion which are in conflict. There may have been times in history when either one may have been more correct/important for/to that period of time than the other. One of them is the concept of the "remnant people" or "chosen people," a "latter day Israel." The other image is that of Zion as being leaven, light, or salt. In the past there may have been times when it was appropriate for the church to be separate from the rest of the world, called out from Babylon, and intent upon producing a pure and righteous people. There may have been times when it was appropriate and important for the people to be able to "flee to Zion" in order to escape the certain aspects of life in the world.

However in our own day and age, it would seem to be more appropriate for the church to give expression to the concept of Zion which is very much "in the world but not of it," as "light shining in darkness," "that the places which they occupy may shine as Zion, the redeemed of the Lord." It is no longer possible for people to live in isolation from the rest of the world; and indeed for Zion to be effective as God's means for "bringing to pass the immortality and eternal life of man," it will be necessary for Zion to be in the world, redeeming the societies of the world. "The kingdoms of this world are [to] become the kingdom of our Lord and of his Christ." For us, Zion must become a lived-out principle that God is involved in and concerned with all of life.

Today as we reevaluate and reinterpret that which God has revealed to us in former years we see the working out of his intention and purpose for us.... Through ministry we have received from the latter-day prophets... we hear God telling us that the nations of the world have a part in Zion, moving to their gathering places and permitting the stakes of Zion to be established in their homelands as the Holy Spirit works to enhance their lives and cultures so that their unique contributions to the kingdom will not be lost. It is important that the heritage of the various nations of the world be preserved in the kingdom of God on earth. This means that the stakes of Zion shall reach out to encompass the world, and that there shall be the give and take, the ebb and flow to and from missions abroad and the Center Place.

Although we can be grateful for the devotion and labors of our ancestors—in the Old Testament tradition, the early Christian church, and the early Latter Day Saint movement—we cannot be bound or limited to their vision or hopes of Zion, especially as those are seen to be either impractical or out of harmony with what we understand of God's kingdom. Persons in other times and places have responded to the hope of the kingdom of God according to their best understanding of God's will. Nevertheless we must accept the task of evaluating those ideas and then making our own response as we judge ourselves to be guided by the Holy Spirit.

CHAPTER TWO STUDY QUESTIONS

1. What is the Old Testament image of the kingdom and Zion? How did this image influence the way early settlers viewed America? In what ways does Howard Wilson's view of Zion reflect Old Testament imagery? What Old Testament images of Zion have meaning for you? Explain.

2. The scriptures state that Jesus came preaching the kingdom of God. How was this different from the kind of kingdom that the Jews, including some of his disciples, wished to see? In what ways does Howard

Wilson's view of Zion reflect the kingdom that Jesus spoke of?

3. Alan Tyree wrote, "Probably for most of our members, Zion is thought of as a community on a sacred piece of geography, dominated by Latter Day Saint influence, and characterized by a perfection of social, governmental, and economic relationships." In what ways does Howard Wilson reflect this view? How do church members in your community tend to view Zion? Why?

4. The chapter suggests that today we are reevaluating and reinterpreting the will of God concerning Zion. What are some examples of this that are given in the chapter? How might some of the alternatives for interpreting Zion have affected Howard Wilson and his campaign? How do they affect your view of Zion?

5. List some community directed activities that your congregation could sponsor. What would it take for your congregation to initiate one of these activities? What would be the advantages of this type of involvement? What are the barriers?

6. What primary learnings have you experienced from reading the chapter?

CASE STUDY THREE

THE JACKSON AND COOPER FAMILIES

The Cooper and Jackson families live in a town on the East Coast. Both families are members of the RLDS Church and both attend the same congregation. The Jacksons participate widely in community development activities in the town. Mrs. Jackson is the president of the neighborhood association she helped organize and Mr. Jackson is a member of the school board. Because of their heavy involvement in community affairs the Jacksons are involved in church activities only on a Sunday basis. Conversely, the Coopers participate very little in the community. Almost all of their activities are centered in the life of the church. Mr. Cooper is the presiding elder of their congregation and Mrs. Cooper is the director of Christian Education. During the course of an evening together at the Jackson home the two couples begin sharing their views on Zion.

The discussion begins when Mr. Cooper comments that he would like to see the Jacksons at more of the church activities such as Wednesday night worship. Mrs. Jackson explains that she feels she can better serve the purposes of the church through her community involvement. Mr. Jackson adds that he feels community involvement is the best way they can help build the kingdom.

Mrs. Cooper says that, in her opinion, the best way to build up the kingdom is for the Saints to meet together as often as possible to worship and learn how to better keep God's commandments. She explains that since God has chosen Independence as the place where Zion is to be established, it is important for the Saints to prepare themselves for the gathering.

Mr. Jackson replies that he feels God is redeeming the

whole world. He thinks God is working in many places with Latter Day Saints and persons of other faiths as well. Mr. Jackson believes that Zion should be a worldwide redemptive movement.

Mr. Cooper counters that the world will be redeemed in Zion only when the perfect society is developed in the Center Place. When this occurs others will be given the chance to accept the gospel and share in its fullness.

Mr. Jackson disagrees, stating that his work in the local community can be as redeeming for the world as the work of others in church activities. He also states that it is just as important to further the work of the kingdom where they presently live as it is in Independence.

Mrs. Cooper disagrees and adds that because of the world situation she and her husband have been giving serious thought to gathering to the Center Place.

Based on the information given in this case study consider the following questions:

1. Which of these families do you identify with most? Explain why.

2. What image of Zion does the Cooper family seem to represent? What images of Zion do the Jacksons seem to represent?

3. Do you agree with the Coopers that Independence has a significant part to play in the process of kingdom building? Explain.

4. Do you agree that Mr. Jackson's work in the com-

munity is as redeeming as similar involvement in church activities? Explain.

5. In some ways the Coopers and Jacksons may be viewed as representing conflicting images of Zion. How does your view of Zion and kingdom building differ from both points of view? What does your view have in common with the thinking of both the Coopers and the Jacksons?

CHAPTER THREE

HISTORICAL IMAGES OF ZION

by Richard P. Howard

Students of the sociology and history of religion agree that the values and meanings important to any religious body have a reciprocal relationship to the culture in which they are expressed. This means, e.g., that such a concept as Zion derives from its larger cultural setting much of its content and style of implementation while at the same time adding to the culture its own unique impact. The purpose of this chapter is twofold: (1) to set forth some of the more notable meanings and images of Zion revealed in the history of the Latter Day Saint movement, and (2) to heighten appreciation for the interrelatedness between those images and the larger scene of American and world history in the nineteenth and twentieth centuries.

THE CONTEXT OF AMERICAN HISTORY

Whenever Latter Day Saints speak of Zion they should do so with a profound sense of debt to the founding fathers of the English colonies in North America in the seventeenth century. John Winthrop typified the prevailing mood of many who sought the New World as a place where the New Jerusalem, the "City on a Hill," that would be a light to the (Old) world could be established. In founding the Massachusetts Bay Colony,

Winthrop and his followers were sure that their new social order would by precept and example renew the crumbling and corrupt institutions of Europe for the sake of human salvation.

This sense of destiny pervaded most of the plans and hopes of the early colonial experiments in the New World wilderness of the seventeenth and eighteenth centuries. Little wonder, then, that literally scores of sectarian communities sprang up in North America during the Colonial and early National period of the United States. By 1840 Ralph Waldo Emerson would observe that there was hardly a thoughtful adult male in his society that did not have in his pocket the blueprint of a new social order.

Joseph Smith, Jr., grew up in that kind of open, experimental social system. Throughout New England, Pennsylvania, Ohio, New York, a colorful tapestry of communitarian life flourished. The Shaker colony at Sodus Bay, New York, was born in 1826 less than thirty miles from Palmyra. Nearly as close had been the "New Jerusalem" colony of Jemima Wilkinson, founded in Yates County in 1788 and expiring with her in 1819. Sidney Rigdon's interest in Christian communitarianism had a natural stimulus in the wide range of communal societies active both in Pennsylvania and Ohio prior to his first contact in 1830 with Joseph Smith and the Latter Day Saint movement. He was leader of such a society at the time he united with our early church. Many other early LDS leaders had passed through various degrees of participation in and knowledge of utopian and communitarian experiments prior to uniting with the Restoration.

THE MILLENNIAL HOPE AS SHAPING FORCE

An important element in the communitarianism of the early nineteenth century was a vibrant millenarian expectation. Through many centuries this hope had been kept alive by first one group and then another, and it sprang into fervent expression in the United States in the 1820s and 1830s. Soon after organizing the church Joseph Smith dictated to his scribe a verbal record of his "vision of Enoch." This later became valued greatly enough to be included as part of Joseph's "New Translation" of the Bible. The portion of immediate interest was eventually published in the first edition of that work in 1867 as Genesis 7:70-73.

As the early Latter Day Saints reflected on the meaning of such a text their hopes of sharing personally in the glorious winding up scene of history must have been stirred. Within eight months of this pronouncement the specific place for Zion, the New Jerusalem, had been chosen: Independence, Missouri. This was to be the place where the whole human drama would culminate in the return of Christ and the commencement of the millennial reign. Though nobody in the church dared predict the precise timing of these events, most felt convinced that the world was in its last days. So powerfully did this image of the "last days" influence the early Restoration movement that on May 11, 1834, church leaders changed the name of the church from "Church of Christ" to "Church of the Latter Day Saints." Zion was to be the societal base for the impending kingdom—and the time was growing short.

The columns of early LDS periodicals such as *The Evening and the Morning Star* (1832-33) were replete with the references to the end of the age and the dawning of the Millennial Reign. In the first fourteen numbers of the *Star*, published at Independence, Missouri, by far the most prevalent type of writing was that dealing with apocalyptical themes. Our church has learned to live with the tension on the one hand, of having a name (Latter Day Saints) reminiscent of our founding fathers' hope for an immediate end to history, and on the other of wondering to what extent such a name, after nearly a century and a half, relates as meaningfully to our present world view and expectation.

FROM TOTAL TO LIMITED CONSECRATION

Sidney Rigdon's presence in the church at the end of 1830 and his trip from his home in Kirtland to visit Joseph Smith in New York must have stimulated Smith to consider the possibility of moving his already persecuted sect to the more congenial environs of Kirtland. Instruction in Sections 34, 37, and 38 reveal the timing and deliberateness of these considerations. By early February 1831 Joseph and his family had moved to Kirtland, and the remaining New York Saints were under instruction to go there as conditions would allow.

On his arrival in Kirtland the church elders petitioned Joseph to seek the mind of God on matters relating to the economic arrangements for the existing communal groupings that had until then existed under the leadership of Rigdon at Mentor and at Kirtland. Joseph came to the elders and pronounced the principle of total consecration of goods. That is, entering stewards were to deed to the bishop by an unbreakable convenant all their earthly possessions of any kind as a condition of membership in the community. In turn the bishop was to lease back to the steward and his family the necessary household goods, tools, farm animals, and land with which to begin the stewardship life in the community. This instruction was written in a "book of revelations" by scribes, and immediately efforts were made to implement the provisions.

As the church later expanded to Missouri and began an earnest attempt to build the New Jerusalem in Jackson County this same instruction was published in the church paper, and was being set in type for the intended "Book of Commandments" when a mob destroyed the press on July 23, 1833. But even before then the church at both locations (Kirtland and Independence) had had legal and interpersonal difficulties implementing the provisions for this total consecration of possessions of the individual stewards to the common storehouse. In May 1833 Joseph Smith wrote to church leaders in Independence to alter the procedure, instructing that each steward ought to hold full title to property, both personal and real, in order to meet those difficulties.

By mid-1835 Joseph Smith had formalized this shift in policy by rephrasing the original February 1831 instruction. This change is readily seen in the following comparison of texts:

...thou shalt consecrate all thy properties,[1]
...thou wilt remember the poor, and consecrate of thy properties for their support,[2]

that which thou hast unto me, with a covenant[1]
that which thou has to impart unto them,[2]

and a deed which can not be broken.[1]
with a covenant and a deed which can not be broken.[2]

This important adaptation to the lessons of history marked the end of the attempt on the part of the church to implement a total consecration. Thereafter, at Far West, Missouri, and at Nauvoo, Illinois, as well as throughout the history of the Reorganized Church, tithing and other offerings and consecration of surplus properties were the chief means by which the church body gained the economic support needed to pursue its Zionic objectives.

In responding to this shift in methodology there is no urgent need for the Saints to try to "second guess God or the prophets" on the matter of relative inspiration. A helpful approach is to consider that in 1831 Joseph Smith sought and delivered to the elders what he considered to be the will of God for their purposes as he understood that will and those purposes and conditions. He did the very same thing, amidst new conditions and purposes, in 1835 and came up with a different set of instructions. In both situations the general principle remained essentially the same: people are stewards over physical means entrusted to their care; their accountability is to God and to each other in community to seek the best possible good for each and all. The only thing that changed was the methodology that most responsibly might express the principle. In this connection Section 147:7 stands out as a clear landmark along our free road of choice in these and other matters.

---

1. February 1831 instruction; see Book of Commandments, Chapter XLIV:26, p. 92, 1833.
2. Doctrine and Covenants, 1835 Edition, Section XIII:8 (modern editions, Section 42:8b).

CHAPTER THREE STUDY QUESTIONS

1. The author suggests that "the values and meanings important to any religious body have a reciprocal relationship to the culture in which they are expressed." Applied to the individual, it might be stated that a person's views on religion have a reciprocal relationship to the way that person views the culture in which he or she lives. What does this statement mean to you? How does this concept apply to the Jacksons and the Coopers? Based on each family's view of Zion, how would you describe their view of the world?

2. What is the relationship between your religious beliefs and your view of the world?

3. What is the concept of "total consecration"? Do you think Joseph Smith was acting within the scope of his prophetic role when he modified this concept? Explain your answer. Can you think of a time when your understanding has matured in a way that has caused you to modify your original thinking on an issue? Explain.

4. What is millennialism? How did millenarian expectation in the nineteenth century affect the LDS view of Zion (in terms of economics, community structure, gathering, etc.)?

5. How has the church's concept of Zion expanded in the twentieth century?

6. Do you identify more with the Jacksons or the Coopers? How do you think you can best act upon your belief in Zion? What can your congregation do to become more involved in furthering the cause of Zion?

7. What primary learnings have you experienced from reading the chapter?

CASE STUDY FOUR

THE SHEPHERD CONGREGATION

The Shepherd congregation of the RLDS Church has been meeting in a rented facility for the past seven years. The facility is located about twelve miles west of a medium-sized college town on a lot in the middle of a wildlife conservation area. There are several small lakes in the vicinity. It is a peaceful area with beautiful surroundings which have provided an ideal Sunday refuge from the hassles of everyday life.

The congregation has set a goal to build its own facility in the next two years. The building fund has been growing and there is enough money available to realize the goal. Consequently, members of the building committee have been searching for possible building sites. After about one year of investigation the committee has come up with two possible sites for a new church.

The first possibility is the location where the congregation presently meets. The man who owns the property is a good friend of the church and he is willing to sell at a very reasonable price. The present facility is a very old township meeting hall that would need to be replaced eventually. But there is room on the lot to build a church before tearing the old building down.

The second possibility is a double lot adjacent to the major university in town. On the back part of the lot is a small house in good condition. On the front part there is more than enough room to build a church. The cost of this lot is more than the other lot but the congregation could afford it.

When the congregation held its business meeting to decide between the two sites the members were divided on what to do. About half of the members favored buying the country lots and building there. They argued that the area was peaceful and more conducive to the spirit of worship. They felt that after dealing with the hassles of a hard and fast-paced world during the week, it was nice to be able to retreat to the quiet beauty of the country for church. They also cited the fact that this location had a great deal of tradition and meaning attached to it because of the rich experiences of the past seven years. Many people attached a sacred significance to the location and felt that it was God's will that the church be located there.

The half of the congregation that favored the other lot argued that a location next to the university would put them in a better position to minister to students. Every year there are at least twenty RLDS students on campus. It was suggested that the house on the lot could be converted into a student center for RLDS students and friends. It was further suggested that a church close to the campus would make it easier for students to attend. Finally those favoring the near campus lot argued that the church needed to be more involved in the community. The new location would provide an excellent opportunity for the RLDS Church to impact and be impacted upon by the university.

Based on the information given in this case study consider the following questions:

1. What are the primary reasons given for members wanting to build on the country site? Based on the reasons cited what view of Zion do these members seem to represent?

2. In your opinion, what are the positive possibilities that could grow out of locating in the country set-

ting? Do you feel that tradition and a strong historical attachment to a place is a valid reason for staying there? Explain.

3. What are the primary reasons given by members for moving to the near campus site? What view of Zion does this represent?

4. If you were a member of the Shepherd congregation which site would you favor? Explain. How could the site that you favor best be utilized in furthering the cause of Zion as you understand it?

5. Can you remember a time when your congregation was faced with a difficult decision? What were the central issues involved in making the decision? What were the key factors that finally caused the congregation to decide the way it did?

CHAPTER FOUR

IMAGES OF ZION IN THE REORGANIZATION

by Richard P. Howard

ZION IN THE REORGANIZATION, 1852-1860

One of the first moves of the early interim leaders of the "New Organization" of the church in southern Wisconsin in 1852 was to inform the scattered Saints that they should not gather to any central location until the Lord should direct them to do so. Early in his presidency Joseph Smith III made it clear that he would make no move to gather the membership together in Zion or any other place without unmistakable evidence of divine direction. Furthermore he claimed some degree of prophetic insight in telling the Saints that the church should remain in a more or less dispersed condition for an indefinite period of time, and encouraged them by saying:

I know the anxiety that is felt by all to be gathering home to Zion, I see the increasing desire to secure happiness, but things seen by prophetic eye seem near at hand when years may intervene before they are brought to pass.—Joseph Smith, "An Address to the Saints," ***True Latter Day Saints' Herald*****, Vol. 1, No. 11, November 1860, pp. 254-256.**

THE UNITED ORDER OF ENOCH

The dream of Zion as the gathered, isolated community of Saints living close together, pooling their economic and spiritual resources for the good of all, persisted among many of the elders. By 1870, just when it seemed that the affairs of the church were becoming more stabilized at Plano, Illinois, there was a decided westward movement of church members into Iowa and Missouri as well as an eastward migration into Iowa from the Mormon trail to Utah Territory. This intensified the felt need among the membership for the gathering, so that in February 1870 a group of men of some means published in the *Herald* a proposed constitution for what they called the First United Order of Enoch. The objective of the corporation was

the associating together of men of capital, and those skilled in labor and mechanics, . . . for the purpose of settling, developing and improving new tracts of land, . . . to take cognizance of the wants of worthy, and industrious poor men, who shall apply therefore, and provide them with labor and the means for securing homes and a livelihood; and to develop the energies and resources of the people who may seek those respective localities for settlement.—*True Latter Day Saints' Herald*, Vol. 17, February 15, 1870, p. 126.

By the labors and capital of a considerable number of church members the First United Order of Enoch played an important role in the creation of the town of Lamoni, to which moved the church president, press, and headquarters in 1881. And while the order by then had been assimilated into a number of local business trusts, it can safely be said that much of the reason for its founding in 1870 had been satisfied in the decade of its operation in Decatur County. Although the millennialistic fervor of the 1830s had abated, that image of Zion which had been its child—the community withdrawn from the world to prepare for Christ's coming—lingered in the hearts of those who worked to bring to pass a more humane and benevolent social order. The main difference was that practical economic considerations based on a longer view of the whole process became more important. Now and then, however, a poet or song writer reminded the community of its earlier spiritual pilgrimage of the latter days:

This cause shall grow, and still endure;
Its power be felt from shore to shore,
Till saints in joy each other meet
And worship at the Savior's feet.
—Thomas France, "First United Order of Enoch," *True Latter Day Saints' Herald*, Vol. 17, May 1, 1870, p. 285.

The General Conference of 1895 sought to revive interest in the Order of Enoch by (1) affirming that the time was ripe for doing so and (2) directing the Bishopric to begin receiving consecrations of money and property to implement the gathering. But fourteen more years passed without specific action before Bishop E. L. Kelley and the elders at the 1909 General Conference were to petition the Presidency to seek divine guidance on the issue. Joseph Smith III presented to the Conference what is now called Section 128. Paragraphs 5-9 mark a new watershed of Zionic understanding for the Reorganization, to which the church since that time has been trying to respond. Some implications of that document are the following:

1. Zion cannot be limited to any single geographic location.
2. Diverse interest-vocational organizations will play vital roles in the Zionic process.
3. Structuring Zion along purely pastoral or agricul-

tural lines will inhibit optimum Zionic development in the midst of industrialized, urbanized societies.
4. The Saints shall experience real interdependence with their nonmember neighbors as they build Zion.
5. The Saints will be sensitive to the feelings and values of persons already living in areas intended for Zionic gathering.

All of this pointed the church toward identifying Zion with the needs of the larger communities. In 1910 the Order of Enoch was reborn in Independence, Missouri. Several economic-benevolent social experiments emerged from its efforts through the 1920s, but they did not engage the imagination, skills, or hope of the entire church or even a major share of its members in any one locality.

THE CALL OF THE TWENTIETH CENTURY: ZION AS LEAVEN

Our progress has seemed partial, halting, and slow. A major cause for this has been essentially conflicting images of Zion-as-remnant (nineteenth century) and Zion-as-leaven. Our valor has often been discretion in the face of the residue of antipathy of the community toward our sect. Also, the twentieth century has witnessed the engulfing impact on every society of international armed conflict and economic disruptions. Peoples of the world have been the unknowing victims of unnerving technological, political, and economic revolutions. These, together with our own church's leadership crisis of the 1920s and beyond, have confronted us with enormous problems in advancing the cause of Zion. This has been so regardless of which image of Zion has informed our efforts at any time or place.

When President F. M. Smith in 1938 referred to "those religiously social reforms and relationships which have been divinely imposed as a great task,"[1] he was pronouncing the platform on which the church leadership of the 1960s and 1970s has stood firmly: Zion as leaven in and for the world's transformation. In the spirit of that calling church elders in 1970 said:

We believe that Zion is the means by which the prophetic church participates in the world to embody the divine intent for all personal and social relations. Zion is the implementation of those principles, processes, and relationships which give concrete expression to the power of the kingdom of God in the world.—*Exploring the Faith* **(Herald House: 1971), p. 172.**

In a sense the "watershed" of 1909 (Section 128:5-9) is becoming a broad network of tributaries feeding the living river of our tradition. Our church had done much throughout its history out of expediency. The composite effect of those expediencies has been to cause us to fashion an image of Zion that defines the goal and the task in terms of Christian mission in the world. We have envisioned the Zionic task to be "the continuing process by which the leavening influence of the gospel acts to redeem society,"[2] and in that vision is the ground of our labor, our theological struggle, and our hope.

---

1. Doctrine and Covenants 137:6a; see also his germinal *Foundations of Zion* (Herald House, 1952), based on radio talks given during the 1930s, for a much fuller explication of this theme.
2. The First Presidency, "Church Objectives Reviewed and Restated," *Saints Herald*, Vol. 120, No. 4, April, 1973, p. 56.

CHAPTER FOUR STUDY QUESTIONS

1. What was the attitude of the Reorganized Church in its early stages under Joseph III toward the concept of gathering? What were the main reasons for this attitude?

2. Read Doctrine and Covenants 128:5-9. What impact has this section had on the church in the twentieth century?

3. What is the difference between the images of "Zion-as-remnant" and "Zion-as-leaven"? In the case of the Shepherd congregation, which group most represented the image of "Zion-as-leaven"? Explain. Which one of these images do you think is most appropriate today? Explain.

4. If members of the Shepherd congregation decide to build in the country in what way could they become a leavening force in the community? In what ways is your congregation a leavening force in your community?

5. If you were a member of the Shepherd congregation who favored locating on the near campus site, how would you deal with those people who feel that the country site has sacred significance?

6. What primary learnings have you experienced from reading the chapter?

CASE STUDY FIVE

THE WIMBLETON CONGREGATION AND THE REENTRY PROJECT

The Wimbleton congregation has a large church building located in a major metropolitan area. The building has several well equipped classrooms, a comfortable lounge area, and a beautiful sanctuary. The main use of the facility by the congregation has been for Sunday activities and Wednesday evening services. The church has rarely been used for congregational activities on Monday through Saturday during the day or evening except for Wednesday evenings. On Saturday evening different members of the congregation clean the church on a volunteer basis.

John Goodson, a member of the congregation, is a practicing social worker who directs a government funded reentry program for people coming out of prison. The program is designed to help people get a positive start as they make the adjustment from prison life to life out of prison. This includes helping people find jobs, holding support group sessions, and providing individual counseling.

When the program outgrew the facility it was using, Brother Goodson went to the Wimbleton congregation and asked if the church building could be rented to house the reentry project. Brother Goodson proposed that the rent agreement be on a Monday through Saturday basis with the understanding that the church would always be available for services on Wednesday evenings and at other times as long as the church gave the reentry project two weeks notice. To sell the congregation on the proposal, Brother Goodson pointed out that the rental fees would more than cover the mortgage payments and the cost of utilities for the church. This would free congregational dollars for other use. He also suggested that this would be a way of using the facility to its fuller potential for ministry. Finally, he stated that he felt the services offered by the reentry project were directly related to the principles of God's kingdom which were so important to the life of the church.

When the business meeting was held to make a decision on John Goodson's proposal the congregation agreed to allow the reentry project to rent the church building on a two-month trial basis. At first, some of the members expressed reservations about using the church for such a program but eventually a near majority agreed to the two-month trial.

In the beginning stages everything seemed to be working well. But after the first weeks some of the members once again became concerned. These concerns were the result of reports from one of the families who cleaned the church on Saturday evening. They reported that when they cleaned they had found several cigarette butts in the trash. This indicated that there was smoking going on in the facility. They also reported that they thought some of the church's property might be missing.

In the sixth week during a Wednesday evening service one of the reentry people from the project showed up and became somewhat disruptive. Because he had just lost his job, he had been drinking heavily. He had come to the church hoping to find John Goodson and help. When he interrupted the service to ask if Goodson was there he was escorted out of the sanctuary by a deacon and given a number to call. This episode created a great stir among the members of the congregation.

By the time the two-month trial period was completed many of the members were ready to ask the project to relocate. They felt that the church was not a good place to deal with the problems of "ex-convicts." They felt that the dignity of the building was being violated when people were allowed to smoke in it. They assured Brother Goodson that they were not against his program and that they were very willing to help in the relocation process. They just did not feel comfortable with the kinds of interruptions that the program was creating. Finally, they argued that they felt there were better uses that the church could be put to.

Based on the information given in this case study consider the following questions:

1. If you were a member of the Wimbleton congregation how would you feel about renting the church building to the reentry project?

2. Do you agree with John Goodson that the services offered by such a program are directly related to the principles of God's kingdom? Explain your answer.

3. How do you respond to the statement that the church is not a good place to deal with the problems of "ex-convicts"?

4. If you were John Goodson how would you respond to the concerns of the congregation?

5. In what ways do you feel the congregation is justified in wanting the reentry project to relocate?

6. If the stranger who interrupted the Wednesday evening prayer service had been a known and respected

member of the congregation, how do you think the congregation would have responded? Are there times when we are more accepting of the problems of our friends than of those whom we do not know? What does this indicate about the way we express God's unconditional love for all persons?

CHAPTER FIVE

ZION, THE KINGDOM OF GOD, AND THE WORLD

by Geoffrey F. Spencer

The concept of the kingdom of God generally refers to the power and sovereignty of God, or the rule of God over the whole created order. The kingdom of God is not yet fully apparent; it is "hidden." Nevertheless, wherever the will of God has supreme claim upon the lives and loyalty of persons, and wherever God's rule is confessed, the kingdom of God is present. The kingdom is present in power, in this age or any other age, wherever and to the degree that people are responding to and being transformed by the love of God. It is in this sense that the kingdom is "among" us, or in our midst.

A new stage in humankind's perception of the kingdom was announced by the ministry of Jesus, so that John the Baptist said, "The kingdom of God is at hand; repent ye, and believe the gospel" (Mark 1:13). Thus the kingdom was present and "at hand" in a startling new embodiment of the divine will and nature in the person and ministry of Jesus. As the early Christian community, and other communities since that time, have received the love of God in their midst, they have experienced the kingdom of God as the power and assurance of God's presence.

At the same time it is clear that the full expression of the kingdom of God awaits the completion of God's purpose, when "the kingdoms of this world shall become the kingdom of our God and of his Christ." This might be thought of as the end or the fulfillment of history, when the rule of God, which is presently hidden in large part, will be fully revealed. Until that time it exists as promise in the lives of those who have experienced its power. The following is a recent statement of faith published by the church: "The full revelation of the kingdom awaits the final victory over evil, when the will of God shall prevail and his rule shall extend over all human relationships to establish the dominion of peace, justice and truth."

The kingdom of God, according to Jesus, is "not of this world." That is to say, it is not to be identified with any of the powers, nations, or societies which presently exist. No social order, proposal for reform, or community can be equated simply with the will of God. Every economic system, political organization, or religious community falls short of the final beauty and power of God's kingdom and stands under judgment. Thus the kingdom of God is present or at hand not only in promise, pointing us to the future victory of God's purpose, but also in judgment, warning us not to give our final allegiance to any human form as a substitute for the perfection of God's will.

God's kingdom is "not of this world" because it cannot be built by human beings in finite human history, or in finite human organizations. Nevertheless, the kingdom of God may be present to us. It is entered by faith and it is absolute in its demand, so that its fulfillment becomes the governing principle of our life as disciples. It is no less real because it is unseen. We experience it as the expression of divine love working in the midst of humankind to change and remake our lives. It is not after the order of human forms of power or influence, but "righteousness, and peace, and joy in the Holy Ghost" (Romans 14:17).

ZION

Zion is the cause which claims the disciple's energies, affections, and will in the response to give visible expression to the kingdom of God in any specific time, place, or relationship. The cause of Zion is the means by which hints and prophecies of the kingdom of God appear in our history. The visible expressions may be in the form of activities, specific structures, relationships, or achievements.

None will fully express or embody the kingdom, though they may exhibit the grace and power of the kingdom and may point toward what it shall be. At the same time each Zionic expression will bear some imprint of human imperfection and frailty upon it, so that to claim finality or perfection for it will be a form of idolatry. Yet the *cause* of Zion, the impulsion to give our best endeavors to the coming of the kingdom, will stand as the guiding, inspiring, and hopeful challenge to which we bend our efforts.

To speak of some particular organization, relationship, or achievement as "Zionic" will be helpful, insofar as it points to the extent to which it reflects, embodies, and manifests the character of the kingdom of God in terms of righteousness, peace, joy, and justice. To speak of such in terms of the cause of Zion will remind us of the coming triumph of God's purpose for humankind, so that we are not overcome by hopelessness or despair in the face of seeming defeat or by the slowness of our progress. Thus the church may properly proclaim the gospel of the kingdom both as a present reality and as a future hope for the world.

THE WORLD

The early disciples were directed by the Lord to "go into all the world." This may be understood in geographic terms—that is, the disciples were to penetrate every land or culture where the opportunities arise. Thus the Christian faith was from the very first evangelistic and outreaching, rather than exclusive.

It may be even more helpful to think of the "world," not as places or nations but in terms of the range of experiences and activities which make up humanity's life. Thus we may speak of the world of vocation and work, political life, social relationships, economic systems, home and family, international relations, human rights, and so forth. The kingdom of God then is to be manifest in every structure and relationship which makes up our lives, rather than merely in some limited part of our lives which we call "religious."

In this sense, the whole "world" of experience is present to us in each culture. We do not need even to leave our immediate communities to confront the world.

There is yet a deeper sense in which the concept of "the world" is used in the New Testament. The world is that part of God's creation which is as yet unaware of and unresponsive to the promise of God's rule. God has created the world, and all in it, for joy and community with him, but the world largely fails to perceive its true calling and destination. Many of the parables of the New Testament point to this "hidden" nature of the kingdom of God.

Thus the world is not merely geographic. The world in the sense this chapter suggests may exist among the Saints in congregations, families, societies, nations, or institutions to the extent that the sovereignty of God is not fully known.

The New Testament is the witness to the conviction that God has entered that world in a particular way to make known his lordship over the whole order of creation. God's manner of redeeming, revealed in Jesus Christ, is not by condemning the world but by loving it (John 3:15-17). The ministry of Jesus makes it clear that the kingdom of God does not win its way or establish its rule by the processes common to political kingdoms.

We may ask, what is the relationship of the church to Zion and to the world? The church is formed by that company of believers who live by the assurance that God has entered the world in Jesus Christ for the salvation of humankind, thereby establishing the authority and rule of Christ over all creation. "The world," however, is not aware of its relationship to God. Therefore the church must reveal this central message of the gospel to the world, as well as continuously remind itself of the demands of such a revelation. It is the faith of the church that the God who came into the world in Jesus Christ is sending the church into the world as a witness of this saving event. Thus the central proclaiming task of the church is built around the call to go into all the world and teach or, as is stated in the Revised Standard Version, make disciples of all nations.

This task will form the basis of church programming in the future as it has in the past.

The cause of Zion may then be understood as our commitment to the revelation of the kingdom of God in those places where it is not yet fully seen and embraced. As such the cause of Zion entails the sharing, suffering, and risk which are witnessed in the life of the One who announced the coming kingdom. Maurice Draper writes:

My boyhood ideas of Zion as a place of ease and comfort and safety (even while the world is plagued with unease and discomfort and danger) carried over into manhood and led to increasing frustration and disappointment. It has been with a dawning sense that Zion is called to bear the world's burdens that I have come to find in Zion the most exciting idea in history. Far from the notion of isolated protection while the rest of the world literally goes to hell, Zion is the church's weapon—God's weapon—for an attack on the very gates of hell.[1]

The cause of Zion is to bring about a reconciliation between the broken and separated parts of the social order. The tendency to act as if life is made up of separate compartments obscures the totality and the wholeness of God's rule. There is no part of the world, either geographic or experiential, which is not the proper province of the love and power of God. Wherever some part of the world is opened up to an awareness and an expression of the divine will, the cause of Zion is manifested. Thus the church, which is the community of disciples committed to the rule of God, and *Zion*, which is its concrete witness, may be understood as *means*. The *kingdom of God* is to be understood as the end, or the ultimate purpose, toward which we move.

---

1. Maurice L. Draper, "The Zionic Evangel," *Zion Building*, Richard Hughes (Independence, Mo.: Herald House, 1978), p. 57.

CHAPTER FIVE STUDY QUESTIONS

1. How does the chapter distinguish between the kingdom of God and Zion? What are your reactions to these distinctions?

2. The author of the chapter says, "The cause of Zion is to bring about the reconciliation between the broken and separated parts of the social order." How would you relate this statement to the situation in the Wimbleton congregation case study?

3. When we read the Lord's direction to "go into the world," the chapter suggests that we can interpret the term "world" in at least three ways. What are the three ways? Which of these three ways of viewing the world would you relate to the "reentry" people of the case study? What meaning is there in the kingdom for these people?

4. Maurice Draper said that Zion is the church's weapon for an attack on the very gates of *hell*. Are there conditions or situations in your community

that could be described as "hell"? Describe some of these. How can the church that you attend use the cause of Zion to overcome them?

5. What primary learnings have you experienced from reading the chapter?

CASE STUDY SIX

THE MARION COUNTY BOND ISSUE

In Marion County there is a bond issue proposal on the ballot of the upcoming election to raise money for remodeling the county jail facility. The present facility is in deplorable condition. It is overcrowded, dirty, and hard to maintain. The newspapers have declared it one of the worst jails in the country and have been very critical of the inhumane conditions that the inmates are forced to live under.

On the other side of the issue, large property owners of the country are complaining that the bond issue will increase the taxes of the already overburdened landowner. Many are arguing that people who break the law need to pay the price of their crimes. They contest that the present facility is good enough for lawbreakers. Because of heavy campaigning by these opponents of the proposal, the press is predicting a very close vote.

Two weeks prior to the election, Sister Charleston got up at the beginning of the Sunday service in the local RLDS Church and stated the following:

Friends, as you all know, there is an important jail issue on the ballot of the upcoming election. I have taken an informal poll of this congregation and everyone here seems to be in favor of the bond issue. We all know how bad the conditions are in the county jail. They will only get worse if the jail proposal fails. The papers are saying that at this point the vote could go either way. In view of this, I would like to propose that our congregation join the other denominations of this county in publicly declaring our support for the bond issue proposal. Five other denominations have decided to take out a full page ad in one of the local papers for this purpose. I believe that the RLDS Church of this community should add its name to the list.

When Sister Charleston had finished, a long discussion followed. While virtually every member present favored the bond issue, the congregation found itself divided into three major groups. One group strongly supported Sister Charleston's suggestion. They argued that the church was admonished to "be in the forefront" on such issues. A second group objected to the newspaper ad for two reasons. First, they were not interested in having the church associated with other denominations in the community. Second, they did not feel that it was the role of the church to take public stances on secular issues. A final group made up primarily of people who ran or worked for small businesses in the community argued that many of their customers were against the bond issue. They were afraid that if they were personally associated with a public declaration by the church they might lose business. And so the debate went on.

Based on the information given in this case study, consider the following questions:

1. If you were a member of the RLDS congregation in Marion County, how would you respond to Sister Charleston's proposal?

2. With which of the three groups in the congregation do you identify most? Explain. How would you respond to the arguments of the other two groups?

3. Do you agree that the church should *not* take public stances on secular issues? Explain. What are some of the primary risks involved in the church as a whole taking a public stand on a social issue? Under what

circumstances do you feel the church should take such risks?

4. What, if any, would be the impact on the election for the church to take a public stance? What would be the possible impact on the congregation if a public stance was taken? What would be the impact if the congregation remained silent?

5. Are there times when we should keep our opinions on issues quiet to protect our interest or the interest of others? Explain or give an example. Does the church have a responsibility to protect its individual members? Under what circumstances?

CHAPTER SIX

ZION AS RESPONSE, INCARNATION, AND POWER

by Joe A. Serig

Historically, a belief in Zion as the implementation of God's will on earth has been a strong feature of the Restoration Church. Early in its history the Mormon movement equated faithfulness to God with the willingness to establish a specific community to which Christ would return. Church members are aware of their efforts in Kirtland, Independence, and Nauvoo. Utah Mormons continued this trend when they moved westward after Joseph's death. The belief that the Saints had a peculiar calling to establish a righteous community which would merit Christ's literal return to earth was a strong motivating factor in the early movement. Belief in this idea helps explain the unusual commitments which were made by early Saints. Many left their homes, and in some cases families and vocations, to dedicate their lives to the establishment of such a community.

When Joseph Smith III accepted the leadership of the Reorganization he counseled the Saints not to gather in haste. During his tenure there was a change in emphasis from Zion as specific place or places to the living out of Zionic conditions wherever the members lived. Independence continued to be identified as the Center Place with a particular role to play in Zionic development, but the Saints were reminded that they were called to live out their lives in the communities where they presently resided. In recent years, as the church has become increasingly identified as a worldwide movement, the concept of Zion has been expanded to a worldwide viewpoint. Rather than calling upon church members from various parts of the world to gather in Independence as an expression of their belief in Zionic principles, counsel has been given for the gathering principle to be implemented in their midst in terms peculiar to their native cultures. This shift from viewing Zion as particular geographic locations to viewing Zion as a condition which can occur wherever the faithful respond to the will of God has resulted in redefining the meaning of Zion in contemporary terms. In no way, however, has this shift of emphasis diminished the importance of this belief in the minds of the Saints.

Concepts of Zion generally fall into one of three categories: (a) place, (b) community, (c) idea or concept. Perhaps varying combinations of these categories could also be identified for differing persons at various times in the movement of the church. Abraham Maslow, a well-known sociologist, has indicated that people's concepts relate very closely to their needs system. For example, a person who is faced with the daily necessity of finding food will likely see Zion as a place where immediate physical needs are fulfilled. People living in highly combative situations may see Zion in terms of a place of refuge. Those whose immediate physical, health, and security needs are met would more likely think of Zion in terms of personal fulfillment and growth. Persons of substantial resources and with high levels of education would more likely identify Zion in terms of the contributions which they are able to make to society through service, culture, the arts, literature, improved government, etc.

A growing pluralism in the church would seem to indicate the wisdom of not holding any one concept of Zion above all other concepts at a particular time in our history. As a matter of reality many specific concepts exist in the life of the church at any particular time.

RESPONSE

One key idea about Zion which can provide a guideline for living with a multiplicity of specific beliefs is that Zion is essentially a collective response to God's love. Zion, then, becomes a type of corporate repentance whereby persons who have individually committed their lives to God through his son Jesus Christ join in trying to shape and change the value systems of communities. Thus those communities can more nearly reflect the basic ethic of love of God and love of fellow beings in all relationships. Just as the concept of stewardship is a recognition that we return to God a portion of the gift that has been bestowed upon us for the welfare of others, so *Zion is a collective response to the awareness that all of life is a gift from God.* When Zion is seen as a response to divine grace, opportunities for repentance, reconciliation, and expressions of universal brotherhood and sisterhood become tangible evidences of our commitment to God. Within this rubric there is room for diverse particular expressions as we each seek to respond according to our best understanding of God's demands upon our lives.

INCARNATION

A basic belief of the Christian faith and one strongly identified with the Restoration movement is the concept of incarnation. This basic doctrine affirms that God's nature was uniquely expressed in human terms in Jesus Christ. We use phrases such as "Jesus Christ the Son of God," "Immanuel" (God with us), and "the Word made flesh" to give verbal expression to the belief that God assumed human nature and lived among us. *Our concept of Zion is an expression of this belief in incarnation.* If incarnation is seen as a process by which God invests divine nature in human affairs, then the natural response of the church is Zionic living—that is, living incarnationally. Among the characteristics of such a people are those of sacrifice, self-giving, growth, awareness of the needs of others, and community involvement. The belief that God is uniquely invested in human life places a demand upon the church to implement God's will in all the affairs of humankind.

POWER

Another helpful way to examine concepts of Zion is to think of Zion as a unique blending of power, love, and justice. When human relationships are seen as an extension of God's investment in life, we look at power in ways significantly different from traditional uses of power found in the world. Rather than seeing power (the ability to control or direct) as a basis for personal economic or political gain, we see power as an opportunity to express love on a wide scale affecting and influencing many persons. When the motivating force of power in any arena of life is incarnational love, the end result is justice. One aspect of Zion in any of its specific definitions is the righteous use of power. Jesus is quoted in the scriptures as saying, "All power is given unto me in heaven and in earth" (Matthew 28:17 I.V.). This statement reflects his awareness that because he was motivated by the love of God, the kingdoms of this world were powerless to quench the divine purpose in him. This quality of loving commitment is the essence of Zionic community expression in life today. Using power to establish justice, rather than personal gain, is a unique result of (agape) love.

Whatever specific images or concepts we hold of Zion, the ideas of Zion as response to grace, Zion as incarnation, and Zion as the righteous use of power will, we hope, furnish meaningful ways to examine particular concepts. The following additional aspects of Zion, which seem to this author to be significant, will also provide fruitful ground for exploration:

1. Zion as fulfillment of divine purpose in human life
2. Zion as inclusive community as constrasted to exclusive community
3. Zion as testimony of our commitment to Christ
4. Zion as community involvement on behalf of all of humankind
5. Zion as world view wherein all persons are considered of equal worth in the sight of God
6. Zion as divine expression wherein both God's incessant call and God's judgment are expressed

When seen as response to God's initiative in life, Zion holds promise not only of present fulfillment but of greater fulfillment in the future. The belief in Zion provides a firm foundation by which Saints face the future with confidence. God goes before us into that which is yet to occur, just as surely as God preceded us in events which occurred before our arrival on earth (I Nephi 1:65). Perhaps, above all else, a commitment to Zion should cause us as Saints to be a people full of hope. We recognize that the fulfillment of our personal destiny, as well as the fulfillment of history, resides in faithful response to the gift of God's love so uniquely expressed in Jesus Christ.

CHAPTER SIX STUDY QUESTIONS

1. What do you think the author of the chapter means when he states that "Zion is essentially a collective response to God's love"? Cite some examples of a collective response to God's love in which your congregation has been involved. In the Marion County Case Study, if the RLDS Church decides to sponsor an ad supporting the jail reform bond issue, would this be an example of a collective response to God's love? Explain.

2. How is the term *incarnation* defined in the chapter? How is Zion related to the idea of incarnation? In what ways could your congregation become a living expression of God's redeeming love?

3. How is the concept of power related to Zion in the chapter? What are some examples of the righteous use of power? What kind of power does your congre-

gation have in your community? How can this power be expressed Zionically?

4. How do you think the RLDS Church in the Marion County Case Study could best use its power to help promote justice within the county jail facility?

5. What primary learnings have you experienced from reading the chapter?

CASE STUDY SEVEN

SISTER JONES

Sister Eva Jones has been a faithful member of the Saints Church for over sixty years. She joined the church as a teen-ager after attending a missionary series. After graduating from high school, Sister Jones attended Graceland College for two years. During the summer before her second year she received her patriarchal blessing. In her blessing she was told that if she would prepare herself and remain faithful she would be instrumental in bringing about the cause of Zion. This promise inspired Sister Jones to continue her college studies and after four years she earned her degree in secondary education.

When she had finished college Sister Jones moved to Independence, Missouri, and took a teaching position at one of the area high schools. She moved to Independence because she believed that it was the place where Zion was to be located. If she was to be instrumental in bringing about the cause of Zion she felt that it was important to be living there.

During her years as a teacher she was able to assist many of her students in finding direction for their lives. For Sister Jones teaching was more than lecturing on a subject: It was a responsibility to challenge students to be the best people they could be. Five times during her teaching career Sister Jones was chosen as the Missouri Teacher of the Year.

Sister Jones was also very active in community affairs. She believed that in order to build Zion, people had to be actively involved in making the community a better place to live. Among her many civic accomplishments, she led a campaign that got the city to build three new parks where families could have a place for recreation.

She was also very active in voter drives at election times.

In addition to her many other activities, Sister Jones was very active in the affairs of her church. She taught church school for many years. She helped organize vacation church school in the summers. She was women's leader for several years. The list could go on.

At the age of sixty-five Sister Jones moved into a retirement center where she continued to be active in every way she could. Her primary motivation for being involved was always her belief in Zion and the promise that she would be instrumental in its building.

Now at seventy-two Sister Jones lies in a hospital bed. She has had a series of medical problems and she is aware that she has very little time to live. She feels very discouraged, not because she is dying but because in her view, her hope that she would help build Zion has not been realized. Zion as she anticipated it has not come to pass. In her despair she is experiencing the feeling that all of her life's work has fallen short of the mark. She wonders why God would have told her she would live to see Zion if in fact she would not. In the last days of her life, Sister Jones is facing her most difficult crisis in faith.

Based on the information given in the case study related to Sister Jones, consider the following questions:

1. If you were visiting Sister Jones in the hospital, in what ways would you try to help her deal with the despair stemming from her belief that she will not live to see Zion?

2. From what you have read about Sister Jones, do you think she has been instrumental in bringing about

the cause of Zion? If not, why not? If so, in what ways?

3. From what you know about Sister Jones, how would you describe the Zion she is hoping for? How does this description of Zion correspond to the way you invision it?

4. If Sister Jones had not joined the Saints Church, but had lived her life as a faithful Christian in the same way that was described, could she be considered a person who was instrumental in bringing about the cause of Zion? Explain your answer.

5. What activities in which members of your congregation are involved would you consider to be Zion building activities?

CHAPTER SEVEN

ZION AS SYMBOL

by Geoffrey F. Spencer

Some members of the church, both now and in times past, have tended to think of Zion in very concrete terms. Some have believed that Zion was a specific *place*, such as Independence, Missouri, or the entire land of the United States. Others have added to this the idea that Zionic cities or cultures have existed in the past, even though for a brief period (such as Enoch's city in the Old Testament) and that there would be a certain time in the future when we could again say, "Zion now exists."

Still others have believed Zion to consist of a certain spiritual condition which would be achieved at a definite time or moment in history. They have usually leaned heavily on the scripture which describes Zion as "the pure in heart," and looked toward the time in the future when this would happen.

Regardless of the particular form which persons might have thought Zion to have, whether a place, a time, or a condition, they have believed that it had a concrete form—it could be seen, located, or pointed to as an actual thing or condition. In most cases, persons holding such a view of Zion have believed that although it might have existed some time in the past, it does not now exist, but will either gradually or suddenly come into being in the future.

The tendency to think of Zion as a concrete or actual

object may have some consequences that are not especially helpful to the ministry and mission of the church in the world today. In the first place, such an idea tends to limit our vision and to lead to confusion, anxiety, and disappointment. Church members who are always hoping that Zion will somehow happen in the future, that they will some day wake up and find themselves in a perfect city or society, are bound to be disappointed. Likewise, members who expect that Zion will be located only in one particular place (such as Independence) are not going to be happy or productive members of their own communities. Further, if members think that Zion can exist only when everybody in the church or community is pure or perfect, they will always feel guilty about themselves or angry about their fellow Saints for not achieving that condition. Finally, if members imagine Zion as having Latter Day Saints in charge of the political affairs of their communities, they will find that other persons will not tolerate that kind of power being exercised over them.

The reason why many church members have developed such concrete views of Zion is that they have tended to interpret the scriptural passages which deal with Zion literally. When the scripture spoke of the "city set on a hill" they have generally thought of an actual city, "a New Jerusalem" as concrete as the actual city of Jerusalem. When the scripture spoke of Zion coming down from heaven they have thought of a literal city descending from the skies to be located somewhere near Independence, Missouri. When the scriptures have spoken of the "kingdom of God" some have tended to think of Zion as an earthly government, with a particular territory, and a system of laws and public officials to administer those laws.[1] This, as we have seen, was the predominant concept that the disciples of Jesus had concerning the kingdom which he preached.

In summary, the tendency among Christians has been to write the future before it happens, to want to describe, from their reading of the scripture, exactly what is going to happen and when. The temptation to give literal meanings to the past and the future have limited Christians in their understanding rather than helping them. This paper suggests that the concept of Zion might be more effective if understood primarily for its symbolic power. The following considerations may point to the value of this way of considering the idea of Zion:

1. In the first place, to consider Zion as symbol will enable us to allow our ideas to grow and develop, rather than requiring them to be limited to some understanding of the past. We will not then be afraid to venture forth into some new understandings of how the idea of Zion is to be expressed in different times and places. We will not need, for example, to be limited to the particular ideas of Zion which were expressed in nineteenth-century America.

2. To consider Zion in a symbolic sense will remind us that it points beyond itself. The idea may be expressed in concrete terms (such as a "city") but the truth is deeper than the literal expression of it. When the Saints participate in the Lord's Supper, they realize that they are doing much more than eating a meal; they are sharing in a truth and a

reality that goes far beyond the literal form of the event. Zion as symbol should exercise a similar effect.
3. Zion as symbol can be a source of great power and encouragement to the Saints. If it is thought of in concrete terms, it will result in much guilt, frustration, or disappointment because we will always be aware that what we expect is not happening. On the other hand, to consider Zion as a symbol that continually points to the greater hope behind it is to find new sources of power and hope. The strength of the Lord's Supper is not in the bread and wine which we eat but in the renewed testimony which the experience symbolizes and points to.
4. To treat Zion as a symbol will allow us to take pride in our achievements from time to time which are fruitful in the life of the church and its people while avoiding the tendency to worship Zion as an end in itself. We will keep in mind that, whatever our achievements, it is God alone rather than any particular thing or achievement who is the true object of faith. We will still be able to identify specific activities, events, or developments as "Zionic" in nature without being limited to those events or achievements as if they were ends in themselves.

The great value of a religious symbol is that it points to the ultimate in our lives. As long as we hold that ultimate faithfully before our vision, we will never settle for anything less, but we will not be disappointed if all our hopes are not realized when we would like them to be. Many church members have created a concrete or literal picture of Zion in their minds, and then have lived in despair either because things did not turn out the way they wished or because they were not able to leave where they lived and "gather to Zion."

Further, if we are to live as if history really had a meaning to which we could contribute our lives, then that meaning and purpose can come only from the end of history. That is why Zion can be a fruitful image; it symbolizes the future into which God invites us. It provides us with a vision and word picture of the future which enable us to rise above and conquer the reality of the present. Clare Vlahos has fitly summarized the value of the use of Zion as religious symbol. Such usage, first, prevents Zion from being reduced to a limited framework in time or space. Second, it relates the ultimate meaning and the human applications. Further, it provides a meaning that can become richer with time rather than being explained away; and finally, it provides a basis for allowing Zion to become the center of our thought and theology rather than just a social plan.[2]

Having made these observations about Zion as symbol, it is proper to suggest what Zion may symbolize or stand for.

1. Zion is the symbol for the assurance of the purpose of God in history. Our history is not futile but is in the hands of God. We do not need to believe that fate governs the future and that we are its helpless victims. The kingdoms of this world *will* become the kingdoms of God and of Christ, though it may not be in precisely the way we would like to have it done.

2. Zion is the symbol that testifies that the kingdom of God is the product of unconditional surrender to absolute love. This is consistent with the scriptural image of Zion as "the pure in heart." The kingdom of God is not material or military power but the life of self-yielding love (Romans 14:17).
3. Zion is the symbol of the salt or the leaven, which reminds us that the work of Christ is not achieved by retiring from the world but by entering into it and enriching it by our suffering with and for it.
4. Zion is the symbol that all things are spiritual in the sight of God (Doctrine and Covenants 28:9) and that the things of the world are to be used in the manner designed of God. Zion witnesses that the whole of life—the material, social, physical, mental, spiritual—is means of bringing the kingdom of God into the experience of human beings.
5. Zion is the symbol which points to the possibility of redeeming not only individuals within our society but redeeming persons in community. In this connection the principle of the gathering encourages us to bring our resources of persons, possessions, and skills together in ways that increase the effectiveness of our witness.
6. Zion is the symbol which reminds us that the purpose of God may transcend all barriers of race, politics, or ethnic origin and that humankind is blessed and enriched by the particular gifts that people of all cultures bring to their association. Thus it is not a matter of one race or culture going out to take their gifts to everybody else; rather it is a process of sharing the gifts which each has.

It is important to say that if Zion is to remain alive and powerful as a symbol, it will need to be constantly reevaluated and infused with new meanings. Some symbols rise and fall; they are born and die because their usefulness and power are limited to a particular time and a particular set of circumstances. Thus, while our understanding of Zion will be given concrete expression from time to time (for example, a communal farming activity or a number of families who agree to share their resources, a program to bring medical assistance to persons who need it, or one person making sacrifices to help another) the symbol will always call us to be open to new possibilities and expressions. Just as we do not wish to limit our concepts of Zion to early nineteenth-century American church members, so we will not want to limit them to our insights of the past decade. Nevertheless, the *symbol* of Zion will continue to have great power and encouragement for the Saints, as it has always done.

---

1. Robert Flanders, *Nauvoo: Kingdom on the Mississippi* (Urbana: University of Illinois Press, 1965) offers the most vivid description of this understanding of Zion in the early Mormon community.
2. From an unpublished paper prepared for use in the Basic Orientation Program, 1977.

CHAPTER SEVEN STUDY QUESTIONS

1. The chapter states that "the tendency to think of Zion as a concrete or actual object may have consequences that are not especially helpful to the

ministry of the world today." What are some of the consequences listed in the chapter? How do you react to this list of consequences? What consequences did this view of Zion have for Sister Jones?

2. What advantages are there to understanding Zion in symbolic terms? What are the disadvantages? How might thinking about Zion in this way help Sister Jones to understand the value of her own life? In what way might viewing Zion as symbolic benefit your congregation?

3. The author of this chapter suggests several ideas that Zion might symbolize. Which of these appeals to you most? Why? Does viewing Zion symbolically mean that we cannot think of it as having any tangible expression at all? Explain. What symbols do you most associate with the concept of Zion?

4. In what ways was Sister Jones's life a symbolic expression of Zion as it is described in this chapter? In what ways can you or your congregation become a symbolic expression of Zion as it is described in this chapter?

5. What primary learnings have you experienced from reading the chapter?

CASE STUDY EIGHT

MARY DAVIDSON

Mary Davidson has been a member of the RLDS Church all her life. When she was a child her religious thinking was primarily influenced by her parents. When they spoke about Zion, for instance, they spoke of Independence, the end of the world, and the second coming of Christ. Consequently, Mary's earliest images of Zion were of a place to which Latter Day Saints would flee during World War III to be protected by God while all of the wicked were being destroyed.

When Mary got older she began attending youth camps where her ideas about religion were expanded. The primary influence on her thinking during this period was the church appointee who was assigned to the area. He explained that Zion would be established in many places. Church members were called to gather together throughout the world to built up the stakes of Zion. This view of Zion caused Mary to believe that as church members developed perfect communities throughout the world, non-RLDS people would see the light and the world would gradually be transformed.

When Mary went home from camp and discussed her expanded views of Zion with her parents they reacted unfavorably. They insisted that Zion was to be established in Independence and people would have to gather there to be safe. They warned Mary that some appointees had "funny" new ideas. She needed to be careful not to be misled.

At the age of eighteen Mary entered Graceland College where once again her religious views were expanded. During her years at Graceland she was exposed to the idea that God was working with many people in many places and that God's purposes were being furthered by many groups. When she shared this thinking with the appointee who had taught her at camp, the appointee assured Mary that there was only one true church through which God was working and that was the RLDS Church. He warned her against placing too much stock in what she was told about religion at Graceland.

When Mary finished Graceland she decided to go to seminary. She was becoming increasingly interested in religion and she wanted to learn more. When she announced her decision she got a variety of reactions. Her appointee friend warned her that seminary would ruin her belief system. Her parents could not understand why a female should be going to seminary instead of settling down with a nice church boy and starting a family. Her professors at Graceland warned that there were very few, if any, career possibilities that would develop as a result of her seminary work. But with all of the concerns expressed, Mary decided to go anyway.

During her years in seminary, Mary had to deal with many new ideas that challenged her religious views. Often she found dealing with new ideas very painful. But as she progressed, she gained new understandings. Once again she discovered that her religious views were changing.

She now began to view Zion as a symbol of God's love for all persons. She saw Zion as an ongoing process with which people became involved at various points in history as they attempted to corporately express the meaning of God's love. She felt that those of each new age were called to seek their own unique expression of Zion, reflecting the culture out of which they came. In Mary's opinion, the form Zion took was not nearly as important as the purpose for which it was pursued. Mary felt that Zion must always have a redemptive purpose that called people to reach out and to affirm the worth of all persons.

When Mary got out of seminary and began sharing her views on issues such as Zion, she was discouraged to discover that many people thought her ideas were out of line. Others dismissed her thinking because they did not understand it. Mary began feeling that there were very few places in the church where she could openly share her thoughts without having people accuse her of trying to undermine the basic principles of the Restoration. Mary loved the church and the people in it. She believed that the RLDS Church had much to offer and she was committed to being a part of the movement. For these reasons she felt the need to encourage people to expand their views on such issues as Zion. But the more she tried the more she was treated as a threat. Mary began to wonder if, given her current religious views, there was any place in the church for her.

Based on the information given in this case study consider the following questions:

1. Of the at least four views of Zion to which Mary was exposed, which do you most identify with? Why do you think people who disagreed with Mary when she presented a new thought warned her about listening to such ideas?

2. Mary's story is a story of changing ideas that come with the passing of time and the gaining of new experiences. Trace the way you have viewed Zion as

you have been involved with the church. How have your views changed? What has influenced the change? Why do you think change is sometimes painful?

3. Do you think Mary should have attended seminary? Explain. Does Mary have a right to express her views within the church? Explain. Do you think Mary's current views are contradictory to the beliefs of the church? Explain. Why do you think Mary is viewed as a threat by some members?

4. If you were Mary and you felt a responsibility to express ideas in the church that you knew would be unpopular, what would you do? Why?

CHAPTER EIGHT

ZION AS PROCESS

by Geoffrey F. Spencer

The tendency to freeze ideas of Zion at a certain stage in history may not be helpful to the mission of the church. Often it has been assumed that those ideas and concepts which developed when the Restoration movement was first established should apply to all times and places. Rather it might be fruitful to understand Zion in terms of some basic principles, especially as these are demonstrated in the ministry of the Christ. Maurice Draper has written:

> We need to keep in mind that the past 150 years have brought enormous changes in human life and world conditions. Emphases in the latter-day Scriptures are related to these conditions. Withdrawal from the world may have been feasible in a rural society of a century and a half ago when isolated communities could be largely self-sufficient. A communal cutoff from the world is unthinkable in today's urban society in which interdependence is an absolute necessity. This is a fact of life which we cannot escape. But it is even more important to note that *isolation and withdrawal are contrary to the redemptive mission of Zion.* Jesus described the kingdom of God as leaven hidden in the meal. This is anything but isolation. It is penetration, interaction, and participation, for the purpose of changing the very substance of the social order of which it is a part.[1]

Any description or picture of Zion will be incomplete. It will be less than the full and perfect expression of God's rule which awaits the coming of the kingdom of

God. From time to time some have set up some organization, or developed some concept, and then insisted that such was the "true" form of Zion. Inevitably such ventures have led to disappointment and disillusionment. Walter Johnson has written, "The dynamic nature of life will never permit us to establish a system which will meet the needs of the community and at the same time remain static and unchanging."[2]

Christians have held different views about history. Some have believed that human history could not be redeemed, that any effort to lift up the condition of the human race was futile. Others have believed that history was going nowhere, or that it was governed by fate before which the human race was helpless. Others have believed that the condition of life would gradually deteriorate until a sudden intervention by God would save those of the human race who had been righteous.

The view expressed in this paper is that Zion is the hope which rescues history from fate or from despair. This is not to suggest that human beings of their own power and skill can bring the kingdom of God to pass. But it is to affirm that history is moving in a direction, and that the end of history, or its purpose, is to be fulfilled in the will of God. Further, persons are called to participate with God in the redeeming of the world. As the reference from Maurice Draper indicated, persons committed to Christ do not just stand by, or retire to some safe refuge, while the rest of the world heads toward an inevitable destruction. Zion is the name we give to those expressions of the divine will in the midst of human affairs which are made possible through disciples committed to the coming kingdom.

Thus Zion may be understood as a *process*. Process has been defined as "a continuing development involving many changes." The term "Zionic process" allows us to express the concept of an ever increasing response to the revelation of God in Christ. Duane Couey expressed this point of view in an article entitled "Theological Understandings":

> Zion viewed as process can be that meaning of God and personhood which gives substance to a culture. Any one understanding of the central Christian revelation, regardless of how authoritative it may claim to be, really represents only an approximation of the meaning of that revelation. The culture of people can reflect only an approximation of that religious experience which gives it meaning. In an ideal sense, a perfection of that process might be called truly Zionic community. There is a sense in which a community where the Zionic leaven is active may increasingly reveal the meaning of its life. This can never be understood as a static incident which is somehow isolated from the process or the stream which itself is dynamic. Every increasing level of the appreciation of the revelation of God in Christ and its meaning subsequently alters the way in which people participate in the process and for them redefines the way in which the *leaven* can become operative.[3]

Communities in which persons are mutually committed with Christ to assist in the reconciling acts of God are participating in the Zionic process. Every new insight about God and God's involvement in the world helps communities of persons to increase their responses to the ministry of Christ. The process of continuing revelation and the resulting possibilities for growth enhance the efforts of humankind to fulfill its inborn potential.

There are several implications which follow if Zion is seen as process. In the first place, we cannot think of

Zionic achievement as static, so that at any moment we can say that Zion has arrived and shall not be changed thereafter. Second, while we will be grateful for earlier understandings and expressions of Zionic endeavor, we shall not necessarily be limited by them. It will be necessary to take into account new situations and conditions as they emerge upon the stage of history. Each generation and each culture will be responsible for a creative attempt to develop the understandings and responses appropriate to that time and place.

Again, we will need to be alert to new manifestations of God's power, not only in the church, but among the nations of the world. God's grace may be expressed in many places and in unexpected ways. At the same time we will need to exercise a discriminating judgment upon the ideas, procedures, and organizations which seem at any particular time to be most effectively supporting the cause of Zion. We will strive to avoid being carried away by innovations that are passing fads, or holding on to forms long past the time of their usefulness.

When church members have expected Zion to come suddenly and fully, they have been tragically disappointed because their hopes were not realized. A more fruitful view might be the one expressed in these words: "It is perhaps not so important at what point in the development of God's purposes we are allowed to work. It is essential that we shall be involved with God in the particular period of life and in the sphere where our lot is cast."[4]

The Basic Beliefs Committee of the church some years ago concluded its statement about Zion with these words:

Zion is not limited to one place or to one period of time. It is the expression of the people of God as they live out the divine will here on earth. Zion is the concrete and tangible expression of the gospel of Jesus Christ. It is the way the incarnation shall be expressed in the world by the body of the church, which not only lives in the world as a signal community but takes upon itself the sins of the world and carries the burden of the world as Christ likewise carried those sins and burdens for our sake. Zion is the living expression of Paul's instruction to the Roman saints when he said:

"I beseech you therefore, brethren, by the mercies of God, that ye present your bodies a living sacrifice, acceptable unto God, which is your reasonable service. And be not conformed to this world; but be ye transformed by the renewing of your mind, that ye may prove what is that good, and acceptable, and perfect, will of God."—Romans 12:1-2.[5]

The transformation spoken of by the apostle Paul is not fully achieved suddenly. Nor can we expect that at some time in the future, by some miraculous intervention, God will solve all our problems or remove all our challenges or make us into the kind of persons we have not committed ourselves to becoming.

Our trust is in God and in his kingdom. We may rejoice in every new insight and success, while still remembering that no human achievement fully reveals God's ultimate purpose. Both as individuals and as the church committed to the cause of Zion, we will count not ourselves "to have apprehended," but "forgetting those things which are behind, and reaching forth unto those things which are to come," We will "press toward the mark for the prize of the high calling of God in Christ Jesus" (Philippians 3:13-14).

1. Maurice Draper, from the study course entitled *Onward to Zion*, Herald House, 1970, pp. 6-7.
2. Walter Johnson, "Zionic Outreach" in *Readings on Concepts of Zion*, ed. by Paul Wellington (Independence: Herald House, 1973), p. 95.
3. Duane Couey, "Theological Understandings" in *Commission*, January, 1976, p. 21.
4. Duane Couey, "Evangelistic Imperatives" in *Commission*, January, 1976, p. 27. The article was originally presented as a paper at the Evangelism Seminar held in June, 1971.
5. Basic Beliefs Committee, *Exploring the Faith* (Independence: Herald House, 1970), p. 180.

CHAPTER EIGHT STUDY QUESTIONS

1. How is the term "Zionic process" defined in the chapter? In what sense does the story of Mary Davidson represent the basic principles of "process" as it is defined by the chapter? Do you feel that it is helpful to understand Zion as a process? Explain.

2. According to the chapter, what are the implications that follow if Zion is seen as process? What is your reaction to the implications? In what ways does Mary Davidson's current thinking on Zion reflect the implication of viewing Zion as process?

3. What circumstances cause you to consider new ideas related to your religious beliefs? What new circumstances or conditions are arising in the world (as you experience it in your community) that call for new expressions of Zion or some new responses from the church?

4. Are there any signs of God's love and action visible in the community round about you? What are they? How can your congregation help support God's love and action within the community?

5. Whether you agree with Mary Davidson's views or not, do you think it is important for her to continue to consider new ideas about Zion? Explain. Do you find that you seek understandings about your beliefs? Do new understandings ever cause your beliefs to change? Explain.

6. What primary learnings have you experienced from reading the chapter?

CASE STUDY NINE

SAM JONES

Sam Jones is a successful businessman in a small midwestern town. Because of his extensive involvement in community affairs he is well respected by those who know him. Sam also serves as the presiding elder of a small and struggling RLDS Church in the town.

For some years the local town government has been the subject of a great deal of suspicion. Many people feel that it is corrupt and poorly run. A recent scandal involving a land deal has raised even greater public concern.

To combat the apparent corruption in the town government, a group of local business people approach Sam Jones and ask him to run for mayor. Because of Sam's continued involvement and interest in the community they are confident that he is qualified for the position. They are also confident that Sam's public image as a good and honest man will bring him enough support to win the election.

Sam is very tempted to accept the invitation to run for mayor. Not only does he view this as an opportunity to clean up the corruption in local government but also an opportunity to initiate programs and bring about reforms that will make the community a better place to live. On the other hand, Sam knows that if he chooses to run his church involvement will be cut considerably. He will have to resign as presiding elder and his attendance at church activities will probably be reduced. Sam also realizes how much the congregation depends on him. He is currently the only RLDS elder in the community. There are young people in the congregation with leadership potential but they are very much involved in starting families and new careers. Sam wonders if any of the potential leaders would be ready or willing to take over.

After considering all of the pros and cons of running for mayor, Sam decides to put the matter to the congregation for their reactions. The reactions are mixed. Some feel that Sam will be deserting the church if he resigns as presiding elder to run for public office. Others feel that the town needs a mayor like Sam. They see serving in public office as an important way to serve God as well as people. But these people do not see any alternative leaders for the congregation and they feel that the life of the church is more important than local politics. They suggest to Sam that there must be some other good person to run for mayor. A final group agrees that serving as mayor is an important opportunity to serve both the principles of the church and the people of the town. This group views community involvement by members of the church as a high priority. While they are also concerned about the leadership problem in the congregation, they see Sam's resignation as a way to force others to rise to the occasion.

After listening to all of the feelings of the congregation, Sam informs the members that if he runs for mayor he will need all of the support from them that he can get. He assures the congregation that deciding to run for mayor would not mean that he was turning his back on the church. On the contrary, he views this as his opportunity to be the church in the world. He concludes by making it clear that he is not asking for voting or campaigning support but for the moral support of the members. He sees their moral support as a way for the congregation also to be involved in ministering to the larger community.

Based on the information given in this case study consider the following questions:

1. Often we are faced with choices that are not always clear-cut. Many times two alternatives may have equal value. Do you think this is the case with the decision that Sam Jones is making? In what way? On what basis do you think Sam should make his decision?

2. When Sam presented his problem to the congregation what were the reactions? With which reaction do you most identify? Why?

3. Do you agree with Sam Jones that being mayor is his opportunity to be the church in the world? Explain. Do you agree that by giving Sam moral support in his role as mayor the congregation will also share in a ministry to the larger community? Explain.

4. Can you think of times when you have had to choose between church involvement and community involvement? Explain. When you have chosen community involvement, have the members of your congregation supported you? In what ways?

5. If you were in Sam Jones's position or in a similar position what would you do? Explain. If Sam Jones decided to run for mayor and you were a member of the congregation, how would you suggest the church handle the leadership problem?

CHAPTER NINE

ZION AS A STEWARDSHIP RESPONSE

by Geoffrey F. Spencer

Nowhere did Jesus more truly reveal the nature of his ministry than in the course of his prayer in the Garden of Gethsemane when he said, "Father, for their sakes I sanctify myself" (John 17:19). Such an affirmation by the one who came to preach and to bear witness of the kingdom helps us to understand the nature of our response to the cause of Zion.

If Zion is understood as a place of refuge or safety, then little may be required of the believer except to flee to Zion or to remove to the place of safety. This in itself may require little of the Christian in terms of deeper commitments or qualities of life. Zion is considered to be for the benefit of the believer rather than for the salvation of others.

From time to time Zion has been thought of as an *example*. The New Testament speaks of the disciples being "a light to the world." This has sometimes been interpreted to mean that people who live in a Zionic condition will let their light shine so that it will impress and perhaps convert other persons.

It is true that persons who exhibit certain qualities in their lives may influence others who see their behavior. However, it is possible for us to exhibit some qualities without becoming involved with other persons in the world about us. The qualities and talents which are most deeply Zionic in character are those which call us to stand alongside our neighbor and participate in the struggles of life, rather than trying to stand apart from the world and influence our neighbor from afar. The message of the Incarnation is that Jesus was not content to stand aloof so that people would see how good he was. Rather he entered willingly into the world of humankind to suffer for and with it. Walter Johnson has written, "Wherever Saints gather, they must win their way in the long run by the quality and concern of their participation in community affairs, by involvement in tasks which need to be done."[1]

Such an involvement needs persons who are not only committed in their loyalty to the gospel of the kingdom but who are developing the qualities and skills which enable them to share in the life of their communities. A light may shine brightly, but if it is hidden under some covering, its rays do not penetrate to and brighten the dark places.

The kind of commitment of which we are now speaking involves the obligations laid upon us by the call to be God's people in the world. While it saves us from self-centeredness and self-indulgence, it does demand discipleship. Under the spirit of this commitment we cannot be happy living for our own comfort, but must be fully engaged in the work which God is calling us to do in the world. It fuses all of life's activities—be they vocational, economic, political, social, or recreational—into one grand service to God and to our neighbors.

However, just as such commitment is required of us as individuals, so also is the church called to commit itself. A self-serving church loses its sense of meaning while a church that is committed to God's call to serve will experience the glory of renewal and spiritual power.

This is the meaning of the statement brought to the church by W. Wallace Smith, "Stewardship is the response of my people to the ministry of my Son and is required alike of all who seek to build the kingdom" (Doctrine and Covenants 147:5a). This life stewardship is a total concern, embracing all of the gifts and resources which we have received by the grace of God as well as those which he has brought to us through the creation of the universe. Such stewardship will include the following:

    a. the management and use of one's personal resources, both for the enrichment of one's own life and for effective sharing with our neighbor. A statement brought to the 1978 World Conference by Wallace B. Smith emphasizes the extent to which the disciplined stewardship of our material resources has a direct influence upon the extent to which others may receive the power of the gospel: "Let the truths of my gospel be proclaimed as widely and as far as the dedication of the Saints, especially through the exercise of their temporal stewardship, will allow" (Doctrine and Covenants 153:9a).

    b. the development of one's understanding and skills, so that our participation in the life of our communities will be both devoted and intelligent.

    c. the capacity to participate in such a way that other people are enabled to develop their own gifts and opportunities.

Doctrine and Covenants 128:8 indicates that church members cannot completely withdraw from the communities in which they live but will rather experience a degree of mutual interdependence with their neighbors and the organizations which make up those communities. At the same time the Saints have been advised to conduct their affairs in such a way that they can be

— in the world but not of it,
— living and acting honestly and honorably
— before God and in the sight of all men [people],
— using the things of this world
— in the manner designed of God,
— that the places where they occupy
— may shine as Zion, the redeemed of the Lord.[2]

In some instances such a condition as described above may be fulfilled by members of the church in their separate places of witness, where the major burden is upon those persons as individuals. However, that witness will always be stronger and more effective when committed members of the church are able to combine their efforts, both because of the strength of their numbers in specific locations and because of the combined impact of their skills and resources. In fact, while we do not wish to belittle the worth of the individual's life and testimony, it would seem that there are some dimensions of the cause of Zion which can be effectively witnessed only by numbers of persons working in close harmony and cooperation.

This is the principle of the *Gathering*. It refers to the power and effect of the Zionic witness which is multiplied as disciples bring their unified resources and talents to bear in the communities where they live.

The principle of the Gathering requires that we as

members of the church give particular attention to those skills and qualities which enable us to relate both to each other and to our neighbors in ways that are loving and fulfilling. The dignity and worth of all persons in the sight of God will be taken very seriously. This would appear to call for the development of mutual respect, long-suffering, preference for one another, forgiveness, humility, and meekness, as well as those skills which may be appropriate to serving the communities where we find ourselves. Beyond this, it will be essential for the Saints to show great skill in making decisions together and then working toward the achievement of those purposes which are mutually agreed upon. The cause of Zion, if it is to be expressed through the people of the church, calls for a high level of understanding of needs, commitment to service, decision-making through common consent, and action that is as intelligent as it is loving.

As we view our past experience and our present expectations, we may well agree with the thoughts expressed in a sermon by Clifford Cole:

> We believe we have a unique history and resource for the call that is beckoning us today. To be called by God to such an hour as this is a most exciting and demanding opportunity. We are enthusiastic about it. We believe the church will rise to its task. If this is to happen we must be willing to sacrifice ourselves to the mission. Christ has pointed out, "For whosoever will save his life, shall lose it; or whosoever will save his life, shall be willing to lay it down for my sake; and if he is not willing to lay it down for my sake, he shall lose it. But whosoever shall be willing to lose his life for my sake, and the gospel, the same shall save it." Just as this is true of us as individual disciples, so is it true of the whole church.[3]

1. Walter N. Johnson, "Zionic Outreach," *Saints Herald*, Independence, May 15, 1968, Vol. 115, p. 332.
2. Doctrine and Covenants 128:8b, c.
3. Clifford A. Cole, "Our Mission in Light of Today's Demands," *Saints Herald*, Independence, September, 1974, p. 26.

CHAPTER NINE STUDY QUESTIONS

1. What is the meaning of the term *stewardship* as it is defined in this chapter? How does this idea of stewardship relate to the case of Sam Jones?

2. What areas of our lives are within the responsibility of wise stewardship, according to the chapter? What other areas would you add? What areas of stewardship do you feel Sam Wilson will be involved in if he becomes mayor? What areas of stewardship will the congregation need to be involved in if Sam Wilson becomes mayor? What areas of stewardship is your congregation involved in? What additional areas would you like to see your congregation involved in? How can the congregation become more involved?

3. What is the relationship between stewardship and Zion? What is the responsibility of the church community to its members who focus their ministry in activities outside the formal church structure through such things as community involvement? Is such involvement important enough to sacrifice involvement in church activities, in your opinion? Explain.

4. Consider the reference to Doctrine and Covenants 128:8. You may wish to make a list under the title "Things of the world." Then alongside each, write a few words to describe how they can be used "in the manner designed of God."

5. Can you think of a time when you or your congregation had to choose between two seemingly good alternatives? What were the central issues in making the choice? Looking back, are you satisfied with the choice that was made? Explain. In what ways do you feel that God was involved in the process of making the choice?

6. What primary learnings have you experienced from reading the chapter?

CASE STUDY TEN

JAN AND JIM BURNS

Jan and Jim Burns have been married for five years. During that time both have completed their college degrees and started rewarding careers. Jan is a social worker who works at a counseling center for single women with children. Jim is an assistant principal at a junior high school. They enjoy their careers a great deal and are highly respected for the fine work that they do.

Jan and Jim do not presently have children. They are both very fond of youngsters and they have often discussed the possibility of having a child of their own. Until now they have been postponing a decision about having children because they did not feel they could afford a child while they were in school. Now that they are working the discussion about children has come up.

Jim is strongly in favor of having children. He feels that children can add an important dimension to a family. He also feels that he and Jan will make good parents.

Jan, on the other hand, is not so sure. She is concerned about the world situation. She wonders if it is right to bring a child into a world where overpopulation is an increasing problem and the threat of total destruction by nuclear war is ever present. She is concerned about what might be ahead for a child. Jan wonders if it is fair to bring new life into such a world.

Jim agrees with Jan that there are problems in the world. But he believes that it is important to have faith in the possibilities for the future. He believes that since God is involved in history, there is always cause for hope. In Jim's opinion rearing a child in today's world is a way of investing in the future. Jim believes that people like him and Jan can make an impact on the future by rearing their children with faith in God and commitment to making the world a better place.

Jan reminds Jim that she works with women every day who have children that they are struggling to rear on their own. She also reminds Jim that the divorce rate now affects approximately one out of every three marriages. She has seen what a broken marriage can do to children and she would not want that to happen to her own child.

Jim agrees that divorce is always a potential problem and that there is never a guarantee on a marriage. But he feels that people have to be willing to take risks based on faith in order to grow. He assures Jan that he has faith in their future as a couple.

Jan next raises the issue of their careers. She feels that her work is important and she is not willing to give it up to stay home with a child. She knows that Jim feels the same way about his work. Jan views both of their careers as a means of ministering to the needs of others in a way God calls people to be involved. She wonders if they would be able to give a child enough of their time as parents without sacrificing this involvement.

Jim does not feel that it would be necessary for either of them to give up their work. There are grandparents available who have expressed a willingness to baby-sit during the day. Jim feels that quality of time with a child is more important than the quantity of time. He also reminds Jan that he has three months off in the summer when he can devote more time to a child.

Jim finally restates his understanding of all the risks involved in bringing a child into the world. But he feels that, in view of their love for children and the potential that children represent, the risk would be worth taking. In Jim's opinion, having a child means being willing to take a risk on the future. Because of his faith in God Jim feels willing to take the risk.

Based on the information given in the case study consider the following questions:

1. What do you think the connection is between Jan and Jim's decision and a discussion on images of Zion? How do you think their decision relates to Zion?

2. With whom do you most identify in the case study? Explain why. What are the issues they are raising that you view as directly affecting the cause of Zion?

3. Do you believe there is enough hope for the future to risk bringing children into the world? What is the basis for your answer?

4. Do you agree with Jim that having a child is a decision of faith? Explain. Do you agree that having a child means being willing to take a risk on the future? Explain.

5. Do you feel that Jan is raising legitimate concerns? Explain. What are the problems that can occur when people try to assume too many responsibilities? List some circumstances when it may not be a good idea to bring a child into the world. In what ways could the decision not to have children be viewed as an investment in the future?

6. Often congregations are faced with the decision of whether or not to give birth to new programs or additional activities. During such times many of the same issues Jan and Jim faced are present. Our tendency is to want more children or programs but, as Jan reminds us, this might not always be the best thing to do. What are the central issues for your congregation when the initiation of a new program or activity is being considered? What are the primary factors that favor the activity? What are the main barriers that might block the activity? What impact will the choice have on the future?

CHAPTER TEN

ZION AS ANTICIPATING THE FUTURE

by Geoffrey F. Spencer

In the section entitled "The Kingdom of God," in the book *Exploring the Faith*, the statement is made that "We believe that the kingdom of God sustains men as the stable and enduring reality of history, signifying the total Lordship of God over all human life and endeavor."[1] Lest the meaning of such a faith statement be misunderstood, the following explanation was included:

> To speak of the kingdom as the stable and enduring reality, however, is not to imply some predetermined, fixed order or system blueprinted in heaven and released piece by piece through divine command. Rather has the kingdom been experienced as an imperative which draws [us] out constantly into the possibilities of the future, reminding [us] of the impermanence of all orders and kingdoms but the kingdom of God. The point has frequently been made that for the biblical writers the characteristic "place" of God, if he should be localized at all, is not "out there" in space but "ahead" of [us] in history.... Thus the kingdom of God is the symbol which points us to the reality of the divine purpose for the whole of history. It affirms an ultimate judgement and fulfillment of individual and social life under the full rule of God.[2]

Zion, then, is essentially pointed toward the future. Indeed, it is a description and a hope of a future which does not yet exist in detail or in concrete form. Zion points to that which is to come and allows us to participate even now in the experience of that which is to come. We have said previously that although we should be careful of labeling any specific achievement "Zion" in the sense that it had fully arrived, yet we should not be afraid to describe as Zionic those experiences and activities which witness the love and power of God's coming kingdom.

The Brazilian Rubem Alves, in describing the power of the Utopian vision, has said that it has the capacity to give a name to things not present in order to overcome the tyranny of things which exist. In a sense he might well be speaking of the power of the symbol of Zion. Our imagination reaches for symbols of the future in order to reveal the present in its imperfection, its transitoriness, and its convertibility. The symbol Zion proclaims (a) that the present is less than God's perfect intention for it, (b) that the present will pass away, and (c) that the present is to be transformed and changed.

The Christian faith is that there is another dimension to our lives than the present reveals. Zion as a symbol of the future therefore presents us with an alternative way of thinking about what is to come. As such the symbol Zion opens the way for the transcending of the present. Persons do not do merely what they find immediately at hand to do. Our actions are invariably prompted by some vision of the future. Zion, then, is the symbol which gives a particular hope and substance to our vision of the future. The cause of Zion is the vision of God and of the future of God.

There is among most humans a strong temptation to return to the past, or to want to maintain things as they presently exist, beguiled by what has been called "the illusion of the everlastingness of today." It is with these that we may feel most comfortable and safe. One writer has said that it is as if we wanted to take off in an aeroplane, descend into the sky, and then return to earth where it is still yesterday. It has been suggested that one of the temptations Jesus faced in the wilderness, when confronted by Satan, was to yield to the temptation to become a king in the expected fashion rather than risk the vision of a kingdom which lay in the future.

Maurice Draper has written: "There is no going back to the imaginary glories of a golden age of which we have distorted memories. There is no going back in any case, even if our memories were accurate."[3] The church, as the community of faith, proclaims the openness of the future to the possibilities of humanity under God. A repeated temptation for persons abiding in the hope of the kingdom is to look back to some former plateau of achievement and wish to recapture it. We need to recognize that a past way of life can never be recaptured. In this connection F. Henry Edwards has written:

Men of the kingdom look for guidance to the past, and yet not without some suspicion. Mere repetition of our yesterdays, even the best yesterdays, would not be enough to satisfy the deeper needs of humanity in an advancing present.[4]

It is true that our deeper needs cannot be met by looking to the past. Not only is such a temptation false to our needs, it is false to the total meaning of human existence. History needs to be interpreted as a whole, and its meaning can be disclosed only from the end. A person may invest a great amount of time and effort in a program of study, but that activity can be understood only in terms of the purpose or end toward which it is moving. The same is true of our history as human beings under God's rule. Jesus as the Christ has revealed the purpose of history through his life, ministry, death, and resurrection, and the kingdom of God is its fulfillment. To look backward is to take our eyes off the future into which God is calling us as the means of achieving the ultimate purpose.

Zion, then, is the symbol of that future. In the first place it is a *true* symbol: it reveals the essential aim of human existence. It reveals what we believe we and our world ought to become. In the second place, it is *effective:* it opens up new possibilities forged by the imagination. Persons without such vision become anchored to the present. Third, Zion is the symbol which has *power:* it releases courage to change things. When things seem most hopeless, they may be the birth pangs of the future. This is the symbolism of the crucifixion.

What has been said is not to deny the importance of the past and the sense of security and continuity it provides. Persons cannot be totally cast lose from their moorings. In Western cultures the unusual interest in the past and in personal roots appears to be a response to the confusion of rapid change in an uncertain world. Nevertheless, *change* is fundamental to the symbol of Zion. Zion says that the present has not said or revealed all that is to be said or revealed about God's purpose and the nature of human life. The Christian is not committed to the system as it is, no matter what commendable features it might exhibit. Although we are encouraged to take the present seriously and to participate in the world with our energy and resources, we still acknowledge that our history has a "meanwhile" character about it.

In this connection Duane Couey has written:

> ...I'd like to say that I agree very much with the idea that history and the past are very important to us. They give us a sense of meaning and of rootage and of continuity. However, I would not expect that we should find a great many answers for the tremendous challenges that confront us and will continue to confront us at a time in which the chief characteristic of the times is the accelerating rate of change. I would expect that we would rely upon our historical roots and sense of continuity for a sense of security that will permit us to embrace the future with confidence. But we will not expect to find the answers and direction,... there.[5]

In summary, Zion serves as a powerful and significant dimension in the life of the church as it endeavors to bring the ministry of redemption to individuals, but more especially to the corporate structures of the societies in which we live. Zion is the *symbol* of the future, and as such provides word pictures which rise from the imagination. Zion is our *anticipation* of the future, and as such locates our hopes on what is to come. Zion may also be our *experience* of the future, and as such it permits us, even now, to live in the power and reality of God's coming kingdom.

Maurice Draper has written:

> God now calls us to share with him in traveling further down the fascinating path of improbability. He has been leading us down this way throughout human history. It is the way to Zion. It is not likely to happen by itself, but it is the goal toward which the whole creative process points. Its guarantee is found not in the probability of its spontaneous appearance but in the awe-inspiring Intelligence which gives

order to chaos, which produces the fantastic universe, which creates humanity in such a pattern that we too share in the process of bringing more and more highly improbable realities into existence. It is this Intelligence which we call God, ordering, directing, and developing the system which overrules all the fantastic improbabilities, who declares that Zion shall be.[6]

The church lives by the hope of the kingdom. This hope is nourished by the living experience of the kingdom. Our hope is not the figment of despair or imagination. Rather it is the sober assurance that our lives "are hid with God in Christ," that we live in a trust and an endurance by which, in freedom, we find ourselves impelled and drawn on (Hebrews 11:8-16). In proclaiming the genuine openness of the future for which we may be responsible, and in establishing the climate of love in which we may be embraced, those who are the church emerge as the expression of God's presence and promise in the midst of a world which is yet to awaken to its true nature.

---

1. Basic Beliefs Committee, *Exploring the Faith* (Independence: Herald House, 1970), p. 102.
2. *Ibid.*, p. 164.
3. Maurice Draper, "The Zionic Evangel" in *Readings on Concepts of Zion*, p. 251.
4. F. Henry Edwards, *God Our Help*, p. 232.
5. Duane Couey, statement presented at the Seminar on Evangelism, October, 1971.
6. Maurice Draper, "The Zionic Evangel" in *Readings on Concepts of Zion*, p. 253.

CHAPTER TEN STUDY QUESTIONS

1. What does it mean to say that God is "ahead" of us in history? Can you think of examples from scripture, or from your own experience, that would illustrate this idea? How might this idea affect Jim and Jan in making their decision?

2. Do you agree that Zion is the symbol which gives a particular hope and substance to our vision of the future? In what ways is this true? In what ways do Jim's arguments for having a child reflect this idea? In what ways does Zion give hope and substance to your vision of the future?

3. The chapter says that the vision of Zion can help to overcome the tyranny of things that exist. What conditions of tyranny did Jan raise in the case study? Describe some conditions in your community that represent a tyranny over the lives of people. How does the symbol of Zion help us to overcome those conditions?

4. How can Christians make a positive contribution to society and yet be ultimately committed to the kingdom of God? Does this ever pose difficult choices for you? How?

5. Maurice Draper says that God calls us to travel down the path of improbability. What do you think he means by this? How does this statement relate to the case study about Jan and Jim? Are there some im-

probable things that you would like to see happen within your congregation? What are they? How would they contribute to the cause of Zion?

6. Make a statement describing where you would like your congregation to be five years from now. Describe what it would take to get you there. Describe what the major blocks might be to prevent your getting there. Compare your statement with those of other members of the congregation. Based on an open sharing of these future statements, list those issues that seem to be central to the congregation as a whole.

7. What primary learnings have you experienced from reading the chapter?